This book will ask you to confront the issues that for generations families have been too afraid to face. Designed to facilitate open discussion of inheritance plans between parents and siblings, it emphasizes the need for all family members to discuss issues of inheritance *before* sickness and death ever become part of the picture. But it also goes deeper, offering insight as to why families are so afraid to face these issues. In addition, it addresses coping with and resolving the emotions that arise with inheritance issues during an impending crisis, as well as the most common time these issues are faced—*after* the death of a parent or relative.

OVERCOMING THE INHERITANCE TABOO

HOW TO PRESERVE RELATIONSHIPS AND TRANSFER POSSESSIONS

Steven J. Hendlin, Ph.D.

A PLUME BOOK

PLUME
Published by the Penguin Group
Penguin Group (USA) Inc., 375 Hudson Street, New York, New York 10014, U.S.A.
Penguin Books Ltd, 80 Strand, London WC2R 0RL, England
Penguin Books Australia Ltd, 250 Camberwell Road, Camberwell, Victoria 3124, Australia
Penguin Books Canada Ltd, 10 Alcorn Avenue, Toronto, Ontario, Canada M4V 3B2
Penguin Books India (P) Ltd, 11 Community Centre, Panchsheel Park, New Delhi – 110 017, India
Penguin Books (N.Z.) Ltd, Cnr Rosedale and Airborne Roads, Albany, Auckland 1310, New Zealand
Penguin Books (South Africa) (Pty) Ltd, 24 Sturdee Avenue, Rosebank,
Johannesburg 2196, South Africa

Penguin Books Ltd, Registered Offices: 80 Strand, London WC2R 0RL, England

First published by Plume, a member of Penguin Group (USA) Inc.

First Printing, July 2004
10 9 8 7 6 5 4 3 2 1

℗ REGISTERED TRADEMARK—MARCA REGISTRADA

LIBRARY OF CONGRESS CATALOGING-IN-PUBLICATION DATA

Hendlin, Steven J.
    Overcoming the inheritance taboo : how to preserve relationships and transfer possessions /
Steven J. Hendlin.
        p.   cm.
    Includes bibliographical references and index.
    ISBN 0-452-28476-7 (trade pbk.)
        1. Death—Psychological aspects. 2. Inheritance and succession—Psychological aspects.
    I. Title.

    BF789.D4H4235 2004
    306.87—dc22   2003068978

Printed in the United States of America
Set in Electra LH Regular
Designed by Daniel Lagin

Dedicated to Deborah

And in memory of my mother,
Susan Selma Hendlin Phillips

ACKNOWLEDGMENTS

Thanks to Mary Evans, my literary agent, for enthusiastic support of a book on the emotional side of inheritance. She offered useful suggestions for rounding out the content of my proposal. Her responsiveness by e-mail was astonishingly swift and her attention to detail all that an author could ask for. She encouraged me during a crucial time to go ahead and write the book when she knew I was very close to letting it go.

Thanks to Gary Brozek, my editor, and others at Plume, for extending the deadline before the ink was even dry on the contract to make room for my grieving. In addition, Gary showed sensitivity in allowing me to write the entire manuscript without interruption or review. When completed, he then edited it with a light hand, ensuring that my style, organization, and content remained totally intact.

Thanks to my brothers, Timmy and Ricky, for being part of the drama and thus helping provide grist for the *Overcoming the Inheritance Taboo* mill.

Thanks to those many patients over the years whose stories in altered form may be found in these pages.

And thanks to my wife, Deborah, to whom this book is dedicated. As always: Best ideas, best collaborator, best wife, best partner.

CONTENTS

PART TWO: DURING CRISIS AND AFTER DEATH 127

PREFACE

Losing a parent is one of the most emotionally painful experiences in our lives. I learned this firsthand—once as a teenager and again, more recently, as an adult. At age 14, I watched my father die suddenly of a heart attack while lying on a couch no more than twenty feet away from me. Shocked, numbed, and devastated, I lost my innocence forever.

My mother died a month after my literary agent, Mary Evans, closed the deal to sell this book—but before I had even signed the contract.

Soon after her death, I had to decide whether I was up to the task of writing this book. I weighed whether it might be too painful to focus on this topic for the many months of persistent writing required while going through my own grief and dealing with the inheritance process. I knew from my clinical experience as a psychotherapist that this was *not* the thing to be doing so soon after my loss. While grieving my loss, could I handle thinking about this topic day and night for the many months required to write the book?

I thought I might not be able to achieve the necessary emotional distance to consider topics without my own reactions creeping in. Then I realized that this project could be a tool for me to work with my own reactions as they came up. I saw that what I might go through with my own brothers and extended family could be very useful in illustrating some of the issues that typically arise.

At the very least, my own experience would ground me in the nitty-gritty reality of the topic, which might be useful to writing the book. And it would be as good as personal psychotherapy and healing for me as anything else in forcing me to look more closely and sensitively at the issues involved than I otherwise might have.

After a couple of weeks of deliberation, in which I allowed my aversion to write on this topic so soon and initial seismic emotional waves of loss to wash over me, I resolved to go ahead and honor my agreement to do this book.

Due to this coincidence of events, you will find a different tone in my writing than you might have otherwise. Some of the examples offered to make a point will be from my personal experiences in dealing with the emotional issues around inheritance. And some of what I write about grieving the loss of a parent will also be colored by my own recent experience of being immersed in the process.

Because of this immersion, this was not an easy book to write. The flow of text was interrupted occasionally with bouts of my own emotion over the loss of my mother. As these bouts began to subside, dealing with my mother's estate entailed dealing with some of the same family complications I was writing about.

What you will be reading, then, is not just some theoretical approach by a seasoned professional psychologist with twenty-eight years of psychotherapy experience. Although I will be offering insight into the psychology of inheritance issues, this theory will be colored by my own experience of actually living it as I wrote about it. Perhaps this approach will make the end product more real and meaningful for you, as it has for me.

Steven Hendlin
Summer 2003
Corona del Mar, California
www.hendlin.net

OVERCOMING THE INHERITANCE TABOO

INTRODUCTION:
TALES FROM THE BLOOD WARS

As we were having lunch after a round of golf one day, my friend Don confided in me that he had a problem. He was a physician who respected my experience as a psychologist in private practice, and wanted my help in dealing with an issue that was more than he could handle by himself. His father had died recently and left him and his two brothers some money. His mother had died years before, so Don and his brothers were the direct heirs of their father's estate.

The three brothers had all enjoyed a close relationship to their father. But, as is typical in most families, there is close and then there is *closer*. And in this family, Don was his father's favorite son. He had gained his father's favor by not only following his father's career path and becoming a respected family physician, but also by taking the time to care for his father during the older man's illness in his later years.

Don's older brother was doing well in his career as an accountant. But his younger brother had tried many different jobs, none of which he found satisfying or stayed with for very long. Now in his 40s, the youngest continued to struggle financially and fell short of the comfortable lifestyle that Don and his older brother had achieved.

Don told me he was surprised to learn that his father's will left him twice as much as his older brother and five times more than his younger brother. He was struggling to accept his father's intentions. He felt guilty and was concerned about how his two brothers would treat him as a result of this unequal inheritance. He had already noticed his younger brother making comments about Don "sucking up" by using his medical knowledge to care for their father in a way that the youngest couldn't match.

Don asked me what the consequences might be if he accepted the inheritance as it stood. He didn't need the extra money, as he was already earning substantially more than both his brothers. Would envy end up creating separation between them? Would the extra money create problems over the long run that just weren't worth it? Should he attempt a more equal division?

I supported Don's sensitivity and interest in considering the impact accepting the unequal inheritance would have on his relationship with his brothers. He had been insightful enough to grasp that inheritance decisions like this may signal the "final report card" of the giver. And that the one who got the "A" grade might end up being ridiculed and resented forever for being the "teacher's pet." While I could see that he enjoyed knowing that his father favored him, he didn't want the envy and resentment from his brothers that might go with that status.

I suggested that Don sit down with his brothers and discuss their reactions to the unequal inheritance. I thought he should hear how his older brother felt about getting half as much as Don but more than what the youngest brother was given. And, of course, how the youngest felt about what could have easily been interpreted as his father slapping him in the face.

When he had the sibling meeting that I suggested, he learned that his older brother didn't really care about getting half as much as Don, as he valued the antique furniture that he had also inherited more than the money. But he heard in no uncertain terms that his younger brother didn't like Don's "sucking up" to their father and "exploiting" his medical knowledge to get closer to him. He resented Don for getting a larger share when he didn't even need it.

The fact was their father had indeed disapproved of many of the decisions the youngest had made in his life. Nor could he accept his poor judgment. Not only had the youngest floundered in finding a career, he also had wasted much of his life in pursuit of trivial interests for his own pleasure. He had been unable to have a stable relationship with any woman and continued to be the "black sheep" of the family no matter how much guidance his father had offered. And now he was being given a final "failing" grade by his father.

After a lot of consideration, Don decided to follow his father's intentions. He would deal with the envy and resentment of his younger brother as it surfaced. He did not want to "bribe" his brother to treat him decently by giving him a more equal share of the inheritance. And he believed that even if he did give him a more equal share, the odds were the money would only be frittered away. He wasn't going to take that chance.

THE DRAMA AND THE FURY AROUND INHERITANCE

Countless real-life stories, dramatic court cases, and popular television and big-screen movies attest to how "blood wars" over money and possessions from inheritance can cause enough bitterness to split up siblings and create strain between a surviving parent, children, and other relatives for the rest of their lives. Short of estrangement, harboring family resentments limits trust and intimacy.

This issue has been taboo for too long.

This book is about confronting the inheritance taboo, a taboo so strong that this is the first book in the self-improvement psychology and personal finance literature genres focused primarily on the emotional and psychological aspects of inheritance. One aim of this book is to empower the substantial numbers dealing with these issues with insight and proactive tools to first face the inheritance taboo and, second, to overcome its negative effects.

This book will ask you to confront the issues that for generations families have been too afraid to face. Designed to facilitate open discussion of inheritance plans between parents and siblings, *Overcoming the Inheritance Taboo* will emphasize the need for all family members to discuss issues of inheritance *before* sickness and death ever become part of the picture. But it will go deeper, offering insight as to why families are so afraid to face these issues. In addition, it will address coping with and resolving the emotions that arise with inheritance issues, as well as the most common time we face these issues—*after* a parent or relative dies.

Extrapolating from the Census Bureau data of the U.S. Department of Commerce, in 2001, 3.2 million baby boomers turned 55. Those over 55 are presently the largest group of property owners. Over the next five years, the over-55 age group will jump to 17 million. And in the next decade, baby boomers over 55 will total 76 million. By 2010, one in five Americans will be 65 or older. This enormous group, who are often defined by their sense of entitlement, will inherit most of the $11 trillion that their parents will bequeath in the next few decades. That's just the actual cash and land value. It doesn't even begin to consider the added value of personal property, let alone the emotional attachment to this property.

Beyond the practical and legal issues involved in transferring this money and personal property, how will the inheritors deal with the emotions involved? How will they deal with one another when the inevitable feelings of inequality and injustice surface as a result of their parent's own preferences?

The above statistics suggest that, besides grappling with the taboo issues in relation to their parents and sibs, boomers will also be thinking more about their *own* eventual death. They will be forced to deal with inheritance concerns as part of estate planning for themselves and their own children. Here are four reasons why:

1. For those who have done well financially, their growing net worth accumulated over the years from their own work efforts—savings, pension plans, retirement accounts, home and possessions—all need to be protected.

2. Some boomers have become credit-addicted in their adult years. Their "I'm-entitled-to-whatever-I-want-when-I-want-it" thinking has led to an adult life of extending themselves beyond their means. For many others, bad credit and debt are not the problem. Instead, they have suffered heavy losses over the last few years due to the reversal of the stock market after the bubble years of the late nineties. These

people have been unable to save as much as they had hoped for retirement and will be depending on inheritance from their parents to help pay their debts or make up for the market losses that affected their retirement savings. According to an analysis of Federal Reserve data by AARP, the Washington-based group for seniors, older boomers born between 1946 and 1955 have a median net worth of just $146,000, including home equity. While many will have company pensions to help them, they will be relying on inheritance to make retirement possible. They will be quick to protect what they believe is their share.

3. Once they receive the actual inheritance from their parents, their nest egg grows, as does the need to protect it—not just think about it. The death of a parent means the psychological "buffer" between generations no longer exists to keep them from facing their own eventual death. This may lead them to be more careful in how they manage their inheritance.

4. The heightened sense of their own mortality as a result of the insecurity attendant to the "brave new world" of terrorist activity. And with it, the urgency to make sure they have their own estate plan in place to help deal with a world that no longer looks as safe for them or their children.

As mentioned, one of the themes of this book will be the importance of facing inheritance issues before a life-threatening illness or death in a family occurs. Nobody wants to deal with this topic before a family member is sick and dying—it's just too tough to think about—and even harder to take any action on. Even then, it is far easier to attend to illness than to deal with inheritance issues.

And yet, growing numbers of us have trust plans and wills long before we will ever need them. I propose talking about the passing on of family possessions in the same way—before we are required to.

> **!** The sound-bite way to say this is: "It is better to face this issue when you *can,* not when you *have* to." (A note on style. Throughout the text I've placed an icon **!** to indicate a particularly

important passage or point for your consideration. These are worth a second reading.)

Although personal possessions may have more emotional clout attached to them than money and real estate, this doesn't mean thinking about how to distribute one's possessions can't be part of good overall estate planning. But doing this kind of planning does require facing these emotional and psychological issues as they arise.

If you can think about death and dying, various diseases, the consequences of terrorist actions, all kinds of psychological troubles, and all the issues related to relationships—including separation and divorce—you can certainly face the emotions around inheritance.

A second theme will be the notion that having insight into your own reactions when inheritance conflicts arise can make relationships with surviving family members—especially a surviving parent and siblings—proceed more smoothly. Although it is quite common, it is not a "law" of inheritance that estate distributions must be contentious or that strain and bitterness must be the result.

OUTLINE OF THE BOOK

Part One, "Before the Crisis," will set the stage for approaching the inheritance taboo more rationally, before the drama and fury are set in motion. This first section will help prepare you to deal with the typical emotions and conflicts that arise when you are faced with an actual crisis or death in the family. Think of this part as preventive.

If you are reading this book *during* a family crisis or *after* the death of a parent, this first section will enable you to gain some perspective and cope with your emotions and reactions to siblings with more understanding. I suggest you come back to it after reading Part Two, which will help you deal with your crisis.

Chapter 1 will look at the meaning of the inheritance taboo more closely and why it is so difficult to face these issues before an actual family crisis.

Chapter 2 will describe the different roles played by the trustor (giver) during an inheritance relationship. Some of these character types will be illustrated by an example. You will you find that you (or your parent) will most likely identify with one type more than the others; you will also be able to identify the roles of other players in your particular inheritance drama.

Chapter 3 will expand on the identification of various roles in the drama from the side of the beneficiary, or receiver.

Chapter 4 will continue our look at why emotional issues are so tough to resolve and offer some help dealing with the emotions generated due to parents' inheritance choices.

Chapter 5 will focus on parents' use of disinheritance as a weapon to control their children, and will look at the roles of guilt, shame, and greed.

Chapter 6 will present the unpopular argument that inheritance is *not* your birthright. It will discuss how your reactions to your parents' choices are altered if you can accept this position, rather than believe they owe you something. How does a sense of entitlement by the baby boomer generation influence their thinking as to what they deserve?

I also offer insight as to *why* it is so difficult for children to accept this position, that they are owed nothing by their parents. A checklist will help you sort out your own feelings.

This chapter will also look at boomers (and others) who purposely go against the grain of providing for their family and believe that they should die having spent their children's inheritance. The "die broke" argument tells us that it is foolish to pursue "financial immortality" and prompts us to give money to those we care for while alive. Even though this is not conventional thinking, I examine it because it contributes to a picture of the psychology of inheritance.

Chapter 7 will address the importance of estate planning in dealing with potential emotional conflicts around inheritance. Not meant as a substitute for a book on the legal aspects, this chapter will zero in on personal resistances that boomers and others have that interfere with their taking responsible action.

Some of the legal terms and basics that relate to inheritance will be defined in summary form, including such tools as a "living trust and will," to keep children and property out of the probate court and the "power of attorney" for decision making, when you can no longer make financial and health decisions for yourself.

A proactive approach to dealing with your estate will put you in the best position to face the emotional and psychological issues that are sure to arise when a crisis occurs. Thinking about them in a more rational and relaxed way *before* you are facing them is sure to prepare you to better manage your emotions and take the necessary actions when faced with an actual crisis.

While facing inheritance issues before a crisis is clearly preferable, I realize most of you who are reading this book will have waited until you have a parent in medical crisis or who has died. Heated emotional reactions from siblings and other family members will already be bubbling up at this point.

Part Two of the book is aimed toward dealing with the emotional issues that come forward during a crisis and after the death of a parent. One of the key points is that future relationships with siblings may be preserved by having insight into what really matters to you as you go through the inheritance drama.

Chapter 8 begins this section of the book by discussing the various levels of the conspiracy of silence, based on the denial of death. It will offer tools to increase awareness and insight, as well as communication, as you explore your thoughts, values, and emotions around inheritance.

Chapter 9 is one of the most important chapters for those who want to gain insight into their reactions toward a sick or dying parent as well as their siblings and other relatives. It will look at how early sibling relationships and unresolved emotional issues with a parent are revived when a parent is dying. Also, we will explore how siblings play out their unresolved emotional issues in their dealings with one another during this time. It will help answer the question, "How does my past affect my reactions to my family members about inheritance?"

Chapter 10 will focus on the psychology of personal possessions and the emotions we attach to them. This is, besides actual money, the area that is most difficult for many to deal with and that causes so much family bitterness.

Because possessions often carry much more emotional value than money, it is especially important for siblings to understand what various possessions of a parent mean to them, and, of course, to understand why a sibling may fight to have something of relatively little monetary value. This chapter will also look at how parents can, by planning ahead, pass on special heirlooms and the values and stories that go with them.

Following up on the insight from the previous chapter, in Chapter 11 we will examine the details of dividing possessions. You will discover tools for deciding how to divide personal property both before and after the death of a parent. I will also address issues such as power, control, and the meaning of "fair" in the division of possessions. Distribution options and consequences, along with establishing ground rules and managing conflicts, will be included. The ultimate goal is to help you understand how good communication may result in siblings not only feeling satisfied with the outcome but actually feeling closer to each other and be as supportive as possible through a crisis.

Chapter 12 is for those reading this book during the crisis of a parent or relative that leads to death. It will cover the basics of managing one's grief so that it doesn't turn into a more complicated and long-term bereavement. Along with our other components of planning for inheritance, this chapter will discuss the need to verbalize all unfinished business with a dying parent before it is too late.

I conclude the book with a brief review of the main themes and some parting comments.

WHO IS THIS BOOK FOR?

One of my motivations for writing this book was the realization that the emotions around inheritance were powerful for so many families and yet no psychologist had written a book to help parents, children, and other relatives deal with them. In addition, one of my specialty areas is consulting with stock traders, helping them manage the psychological aspects of trading and investing. I have published a book on the psychology of online trading and, for a year and a half, wrote a weekly column for TheStreet.com, an online trading and investment site. So I am sensitized to and knowledgeable about the financial aspects of inheritance. This sensitivity, along with my long psychotherapy practice, makes me especially qualified to write a book on this topic. It also informs my interest in helping you face the financial and material aspects of inheritance, along with the emotional ones.

It dawned on me that my generation of baby boomers might be able to take a step beyond avoiding inheritance issues, unlike other generations that have been unable to face them directly. So the primary group this book is aimed at is all those baby boomers who are or will be facing the death of their aging parents. But since *death does not discriminate* by generation, the larger group this book is meant for is parents, siblings, and other family members who are confronting the emotional issues of the inheritance taboo. It is also intended for all those working in fields relating to the care of seniors, such as trust attorneys, financial planners, hospice workers, nurses, physicians, and mental health professionals.

Parents who need to break through the taboo and discuss their inheritance wishes and the values they would like to pass on to their children will also find this book useful. So will relatives other than children who are dealing with their reactions to an inheritance disposition. If you are one of those extended family members, you will find the section devoted to helping make decisions about the division of possessions particularly relevant.

This is *not* the best book to consult if your primary interest is in the legal aspects of inheritance. Nor is it the book for those who are looking for tax information related to inheritance or advice on how to invest or manage an inheritance. And while it will offer a chapter for those who are grieving the loss of a parent, it will not be as thorough as a book focused solely on grieving.

The good news is that there are plenty of books on the legal aspects of inheritance as well as on grieving your loss. The bad news is that, up until this book, you could find very little in the way of help for the emotional side of the issue, *either before or during* the process itself. The literature on how to go about dividing possessions, for example, is sparse and unknown. In this book, I will take you step by step through this process.

For all those looking for insight and guidance on the psychological and emotional entanglements that are unique to families when it comes time to face inheritance, this book will not only help clarify the issues but offer various solutions to help make the process less painful.

I make an unpleasant and easily avoided topic one you can stay interested in, not push it aside because of the emotions that may arise while reading, by giving a number of interesting stories related to inheritance. These tales will both illustrate the various points I'm trying to make as well as capture your interest. The truth is, when it comes to inheritance, although we each wish to avoid ending up as just another tale of greed and family resentment, many of us will read with interest as long as it's the *other guy's* intriguing story being told.

In addition, it's sometimes easier to take in information that is emotionally charged (because you are identifying with the material) by distancing yourself somewhat as you are reading.

The stories are intended to help you distance yourself *just enough* to separate yourself from the drama but, at the same time, get the message and then apply it to your own situation, if it fits.

PART ONE:
BEFORE THE CRISIS

CHAPTER 1
THE INHERITANCE TABOO

Reena, 28, stormed into my office seething with rage. For the first twenty minutes of her psychotherapy session, she spewed out a torrent of angry venom toward the "evil bitch" who was now her stepmother. She blamed this woman for "twisting" her father's mind. Her father, in his mid-50s, had remarried about a year after Reena's mother died in a car crash. He'd now been married for two years but the fury of Reena's anger made it clear that the issue was still very much on the front burner—and the burner was turned up high.

From the time Reena had been a teenager, her mother promised her that when she died, Rena would inherit her pearl necklace. The necklace was one of her mother's prized possessions, as it had been given to her by her own mother. Besides the monetary value due to the quality of the pearls, it held a lot of emotional meaning to Reena. But it had never been written down in her mother's will that the necklace would go to Reena. Her mother was only in her early 50s; no one ever imagined she would die so young. Like so many, she never thought a list of how to dispose of her possessions was necessary.

Because of the suddenness of her death, she didn't have the time to hand her daughter the long-promised necklace that meant so much to her, despite her wanting Reena to have it.

Consumed with loss and grieving her mother's shocking death, Reena didn't think much about the necklace at the time. Her father had been physically exhausted and overwhelmed with grief as well. Reena just couldn't bring herself to ask him directly about the necklace.

But in the back of her mind, she knew her father was aware of her mother's wishes. They'd never discussed the issue, but she expected him to give her the necklace when he felt ready to deal with her mother's possessions. Because she didn't want to seem insensitive to his mourning or appear to be "grabbing my dead mother's pearls," Reena held back from ever bringing it up.

Despite thinking he would never meet another woman he could care for, her father remarried a woman ten years younger than himself within eight months. And she just happened to be a casual friend of his wife. It was at this time Reena began to think she would never again see the necklace.

From the start, Reena mistrusted the woman's motives for marrying her father. She suspected her new stepmother of being a "gold digger." Her finances were unstable but this did not stop her from buying expensive clothes. Her mistrust deepened when the "evil bitch," after one too many glasses of wine at an engagement party, stood up in front of the entire family and announced that Reena's father was the "sexiest man I'd ever been with." Upon hearing this, Reena wanted to "poke her eyes out." She believed this woman was only trying to "butter him up" and thought making him "look like a stud" was the way to do it.

As I sat listening to Reena's angry explosion, I knew this issue was resurfacing as a result of the holiday season. Reena was spending another holiday apart from her father, who now lived across the country. She had refused to visit him since the remarriage. In fact, she could barely even speak to him on the phone.

What caused the family strain was a phone conversation she had with her father soon after he remarried. When Reena finally asked about the necklace, he told her he'd given it to his new wife as a gift! Reena was stunned. She couldn't believe her father was going to deprive her of what she considered her birthright. This is why she was so angry at the "evil bitch," whom she believed had talked her passive father into giving her the necklace, rather than honoring Reena's mother's wishes.

But there was more going on here. Although the new wife was an easy scapegoat, it was not as simple as blaming her father's actions on his new partner. I could see that her father felt ambivalent about giving Reena the necklace. He had long resented that she showed little interest in joining the family for gatherings. Reena had made a life for herself on the West Coast while the rest of the family lived in the South. She was a professional who was dedicated to her work and refused to run back to visit every time her father wanted her to.

So the larger truth was that Reena's father was withholding the necklace as a way to punish her for not being a "good girl." Giving it to his new wife was his way of showing Reena that she was undeserving of the necklace. But it took me some time to get Reena to accept this interpretation and not just blame her new stepmother.

The inheritance taboo had reared its ugly head with Reena. The inability of her family to face the death of her mother directly and discuss the disposition of her possessions had cost Reena "her" pearl necklace. And it had poisoned her relationship with her father, with whom she had been so close growing up. Now she wouldn't even speak to him. She cursed his new "evil" wife and blamed her for adding the insult of not getting what she believed was rightfully hers to the emotional injury of her mother's sudden death.

WHAT MAKES IT A TABOO?

Why do I call the difficulty in discussing inheritance issues a "taboo"? It's a taboo because emotional aversion and social custom teach us to avoid it—no matter how devastating the consequences. We consider it rude and insensitive to discuss anything having to do with inheritance. How do family members get to the point of not being able to mention this topic openly or face the reality of it? And how do previously loving family members end up in such bitter disagreements that they become enemies, hating and shunning each other for years or even the rest of their adult lives? Why is this kind of alienating outcome so common? Why is it so tough to deal with and resolve their differences more directly and openly? Why is it so difficult to compromise?

For adult children, facing the taboo typically means accepting the seriousness of a gravely ill parent's situation and the reality of his impending death. Some family situations (such as quick death by heart attack) don't allow time to mentally prepare for death, so this can be especially trying for adult children to deal with. They are forced to react *after the fact*, when the emotions that are part of mourning are very likely to color decision making.

Adult children don't want to have to accept that a sick and dying parent is really going to die, so anything we associate with the actual death, like dealing with inheritance plans, we easily push aside. Parents, the adult children, the surviving parent when there is one, and other family members and friends all practice this avoidance. So even if some members of the family are ready to face the issue, oftentimes one or more other members of the equation will defeat the attempts to raise the issue.

If we do raise the issue, it is easy for our initial discussions to fall short of actual decision making or any action at all. We can think of this resistance to face death directly as a "conspiracy of silence." This conspiracy demonstrates the power of the taboo.

We need to realize that it isn't just that we don't want to accept the prospect of the literal death of a parent. Because we think the reality of their death will be too painful, we block or defend against experiencing any emotion related to their death while the person is still alive.

Let me give you a personal example of what happens when you let a bit of this reality in, rather than defend against it. In the last few months of my mother's life, she was losing weight and was quite frail compared to how robust she'd been throughout her life. She was mentally alert, able to walk and get around with some help, but it was clear that she was deteriorating. She was on dialysis three times a week. This kept her alive but made her weak. But she managed with some help to continue living in her own home to the end of her life in a big house she had been in for fifty years. Over the last half year or so when I would see her, sometimes I would begin to tear up. I could not escape realizing that she was dying, even though she was not on her deathbed and was often in pretty good spirits.

During her first brief hospitalization due to breathing difficulties, I was struck even more forcefully with the clear awareness that she was dying. It was on a Fourth of July afternoon that she went into the hospital by ambulance. I didn't think she would make it to her 85th birthday at Thanksgiving time. She didn't. But when she came home after a few days in the hospital, I began crying softly when I first looked at her. I was grateful that she was still alive but already feeling the pain of knowing her time was limited. I found it difficult to be around her for too long because the pain of loss that I was already experiencing hurt too much.

In other words, I didn't wait for her to die before I felt the loss. This made the time with her more meaningful. But it also made me begin to emotionally defend myself against feeling too much attachment to her—an attachment, of course, that had been built over fifty years of life. I began to purposely lessen my attachment so that it would be less painful for me when she actually died.

To let in the full awareness of loss *before* she died would have been more than I could tolerate, as the pain that goes with the reality of actual death is obviously something very different than simply trying to detach from a person while he or she is still alive.

Although it may sound flippant, no matter how miserable your condition my be, you're not dead until you're dead. And in my mother's case, she was able to live reasonably well right up to the morning she died. This made it easier for me to think that maybe she would stay alive longer, perhaps a few months more.

When we do open ourselves to the feeling of loss while the person is alive, we resist feeling too much. We may permit *thoughts* about the parent's death, but it is more difficult to let in the emotion that accompanies them. And yet, letting it in helps us make more precious the time the person has left while, at the same time, pushes us to resist letting in more than we can manage. To be sure, it's a delicate balance.

Here's another personal example of feeling the loss before it actually occurs. A few months before my mother died, she arrived at a Hollywood theater with my brother and his girlfriend to see a special preview of a play. It was important to my mom to make the effort to attend the preview because the sister of my brother's girlfriend was starring and my mother had not yet met her. The three of them ended up arriving a bit late, only a few minutes before the play was to begin. When my mother greeted me, she announced that her best friend of seventy years had died that afternoon and that she had been given the news just before leaving for the theater. Despite the fact that we were standing in public, ready to enter the theater to take our seats, upon hearing the news, I immediately began crying.

Now, while I had some feeling for my mother's best friend and had known her over the course of my whole life, I'm not exactly the kind of guy who bursts into tears upon hearing news about the deaths of friends and neighbors—and certainly not in public. I can go years with nothing more than being touched, a bit of tearing here and there for a sentimental movie but not actually crying. In fact, the last time that I could remember really crying was in reaction to hearing about the tragic death of the professional golfer Payne Stewart, on October 25, 1999. I was so shocked at hearing about his tragic death that a few minutes later, while teary-eyed, I absentmindedly cut the tip of my thumb deeply while trying to open a can of tuna.

After my mother informed me of her dearest friend's death, I walked away to be by myself for a few minutes and continued crying softly. I knew my emotion was coming from someplace else. And it was. I was reacting not only to the news of the death of my mother's lifelong friend but also to what I associated to it.

Of course, nobody knew this, nor did they care. My family seemed surprised at my public display of tears because they knew it was highly unusual behavior for me. When I had a chance to calm down while watching the play and examine my reaction, I realized where these tears were coming from. My mother's friend dying reinforced my knowledge of the impending death of my mother. I was experiencing a mini-version of learning of the death of my mother, even though she was standing in front of me. I call this behavior of feeling the loss before it actually occurs "anticipatory grieving." I don't know how common it is, nor have I read anything about it in the literature on grieving. But I don't imagine I'm the only one to experience it.

As if accepting the impending death of a parent is not difficult enough, as an adult child, facing the taboo also means indirectly having to face *your own* eventual death, even if you do this on a less conscious level. This faint sense is more in the background than the foreground of your awareness.

The taboo against dealing with death and inheritance directly is how it has been for many generations. No one really wants to face the emotional side of inheritance directly. That is why, up to now, no books have been written on this subject, despite the fact that it is an issue that all families, in all generations, and in all cultures, must confront.

No one wants to talk about it or read about it. No one wants to accept the possibility that you can love your parents deeply and also have frank discussions with them about their inheritance plans. Curiously, having this kind of direct discussion has never been thought of as a loving act. We think of discussing inheritance as an attempt to protect our own selfish interest in money, land, title, and possessions—it's certainly *not* for the benefit of the parent who is dying to help him or her clarify their true wishes. It takes a courageous person to face these issues directly. And yet the result, for those who are brave enough to deal with the issues, may be a greater closeness between parent and children.

Of course, this has never stopped anyone from discussing inheritance privately, away from the dying parent, which is often when the first shots that will lead to full-blown "blood wars" once the parent has died are fired—sometimes even before.

Besides being viewed as self-serving and inconsiderate, bringing up inheritance issues directly with parents has other implications. Many people interpret discussing these issues with a sick or dying parent as "giving up" on any recovery and jumping forward to the parent's death. Worse yet, it implies in the recesses (or forefront) of family members' minds that you are looking forward to your parent's death. Acknowledging the reality of something does *not* mean we want it to happen. This confusion arises when family members can't tolerate these issues being discussed.

Ideally, bringing up inheritance issues helps a parent feel that his or her wishes are being carried out directly by children or an outside executor. It offers a chance for values to be discussed and passed down with an impact that a written will or even a video just can't have. And it's a chance for a parent to pass on to a child the history of family heirlooms, so that we can experience a sense of continuity of the valued possessions. More on this later in the book.

In addition, facing death directly allows us to further the process of closure with the dying person, so that doubts and unresolved issues are less likely to torment us once the person is gone.

Yet so very few of us ever take advantage of this important psychological and emotional concern.

SUPERSTITIOUS THINKING

Another reason I refer to discussions about inheritance among family members as "taboo" relates directly to one of the definitions of the word itself: Something that is taboo cannot be mentioned because it is sacred and forbidden.

Just as superstitious primitive tribes forbade the mention of certain things, today we have the same kind of superstitious thinking when it comes to discussing inheritance. Let me explain what I mean by this.

> **[!]** Believe it or not, some families think that simply bringing up the topic of inheritance when a parent is sick or dying will hasten the event. This is the same kind of superstitious thinking the primitive islanders would use. Does mentioning something like inheritance plans really have anything to do with whether someone gets better or worse? Certainly not in a physical sense.

Could a dying parent take comfort in knowing that his inheritance wishes will be honored? Yes, of course. But this is only going to make him rest more comfortably, with a greater peace of mind. It is not going to make him physically recover—just as discussing inheritance plans is not going to make the person suddenly get worse or die.

For example, a spouse will tell the children not to mention the possibility of death because it means they've given up hope that the sick person will recover. Even when they know the person is dying, they still believe it is breaking some kind of sacred taboo to think thoughts of inheritance or death. Some spouses just aren't ready to accept that their partner is going to die. And they are unwilling to let their children accept it, either. Their dependence on their partner is so strong that they can't bear the thought of being forced to survive without him or her.

This is an obvious form of denial. In addition, it makes it far more difficult for siblings and other loved ones to say their good-byes to the dying person. It also means nothing whatsoever having to do with inheritance is allowed to be spoken of openly.

This superstition is, unfortunately, more common than you might believe. Despite knowing that saying "good-bye" to their loved one is important, they simply can't bring themselves to do it. And they refuse to let their children or grandchildren do it in front of them. So children are then forced to say their good-byes when the other parent is not around, and anything having to do with inheritance plans is not going to be discussed. This superstitious behavior is not psychologically in the best interest of anyone, including the dying parent.

Besides the superstition that open discussion means bad things will happen, facing the taboo also means that the dying parent is forced to deal with the uncomfortable examination of their preferences for one child over another. By avoiding the issue altogether, he or she avoids having to bring these preferences into conscious awareness and avoids having to make painful decisions based upon them.

> **!** Similarly, facing preferences of one child over another also means facing the possibility of having to discuss these preferences with the family and dealing with everyone's reactions. Instead, the dying parent will procrastinate or trivialize the issue and deal with a favored child by

giving him or her money and possessions privately, "behind the back" of the other children. I will discuss this in more depth in another chapter.

Another element contributing to superstitious thinking is a distorted notion in pop psychology and behavioral medicine regarding "the power of positive thinking." The literature suggests that it may very well be of benefit for patients fighting diseases like cancer, HIV, heart attack, or stroke to practice positive thinking and engage in exercises that help them stay engaged in life rather than to fall prey to depression and hopelessness. So far, so good.

But this is a very different stage than when a person is clearly dying. At this point, the main psychological task is to come to terms with his or her death. The problem is that coming to terms with one's death may be confused with "negative thinking," and thus creates an added taboo element to dealing openly with death and inheritance.

> **!** Facing the taboo also means the dying parent must face another form of denial. And that's the denial that what happens to their money and possessions matters. We may call this the "Who cares?" attitude: "It doesn't matter to me where my money and possessions go because I'll be dead and won't know the difference."

Certain personality types hold this position, even though we may view this as selfish, irresponsible, and shortsighted. Those looking for a rationalization not to have to face the issues more directly may hold this belief and so do individuals who believe that inheritance is an outdated concept. These people believe it is better to give everything away while you are alive. We will talk more about this philosophy in a later chapter.

Finally, even when parents and children are able to overcome all the other resistances that have been listed above, there is another obstacle they must face—the reality that in family relationships feelings and preferences can change over time.

A trust or will needs to be periodically reviewed and updated to reflect current preferences or changes in the family structure, and any listing of our preferences for distribution of money and personal property must also be revised, as conditions warrant. The relevance of this concern comes up quite often in families, in that the sick and dying person often doesn't have the energy or interest to deal with revising these documents many years after they were first drawn up.

ARE YOU READY TO FACE THE TABOO?

Now that we've identified some of the obstacles that make dealing with inheritance a taboo, answering the following global questions will help to assess your readiness to begin addressing these issues. Let's assume you're reading this *before* a crisis. All family members, especially the parent in question, the spouse, and children should answer these questions separately and then, if possible, compare their answers:

1. When I think about dealing with inheritance issues, the whole thing feels overwhelming and spooky, and frightens me.
2. I feel like there is enough conflict with my siblings/parents already without opening up the whole emotional can of worms related to death and inheritance.
3. I have procrastinated when it comes to drawing up a will. The legal mumbo jumbo related to considering a living trust as part of my inheritance planning causes my eyes to glaze over.
4. I don't like the idea of having to pay an attorney to help me deal with inheritance issues because it is my personal business.
5. I've thought about how I want to distribute my personal possessions and realize that I can't stand the idea of giving more to one child than another.
6. Every time I think about how I want to give away my possessions I begin to feel overcome by the awareness of my own death.
7. I've tried to bring up inheritance concerns with my mother or father but he/she doesn't respond in a way that invites further discussion.

8. My siblings and I have discussed some of our concerns regarding our parent's physical problems and how to deal with them but we don't think it's right to start talking about his/her possessions or money.
9. I'm fearful that mentioning my concerns about my mother/father to my sibs will only make them get the wrong idea.
10. Taking care of my parent's physical problems seems much more important than dealing with inheritance issues.

If you agreed with five or more of these statements, you need to read the rest of this book *very carefully* so that you may face your inheritance taboo. This book was written with you in mind!

> **!** If you agreed with less than five, you are less resistant to face the taboo and ready to absorb the material presented so that you may take necessary action. "Taboo busters" are assertive, independent thinkers, freely able to express their preferences and opinions, and free of paralyzing shame and guilt that interferes with confronting significant others. They also have higher levels of trust and self-disclosure with family members. However, taboo busters still have to deal with family members who may not share their more enlightened attitude.

Notice how your answers may change as you continue reading. One purpose of this book is to help you feel able to face your family members more openly in dealing with all of the emotional and financial issues around inheritance. Learning to face these issues more directly—both as to how you feel about them and your ability to discuss them with family members—will mean that you are facing the taboo directly and, in so doing, are reducing the chances of being overwhelmed by them or having them result in long-term emotional problems with everyone concerned.

The next two chapters introduce the various roles played by those leaving an inheritance and those receiving one.

CHAPTER 2
ROLES IN THE FAMILY DRAMA: GIVERS

This chapter will help you identify various roles in the inheritance drama from the perspective of the trustor, or giver. The following chapter will look at the various roles from the perspective of the beneficiary, or receiver.

As you read, notice which one seems to be closest to the role with which you identify. It doesn't require a written personality test to figure out which role is closest to the one you play in your family. Even though you may not want to identify with some of the characteristics implied in a role, try to be as honest as possible with yourself as you read.

In addition, try to identify the roles of key family members. In doing so, the psychological dynamics between you and family members may become more clear, especially as we continue delving into the issues that create such tension and disagreement between parents and children and sibs themselves.

WHAT DOES IT MEAN TO PLAY A ROLE?

When I talk about "playing a role" in the following descriptions, what I mean is that, to some degree, you are "cast" in a part by your order of birth, personality, life decisions, and even some genetic traits. Because you can't control all of these things, you may feel like you're been miscast. But that is only part of the picture. Another aspect to your role is very much your own choosing—the conscious and intentional positioning you take on because it satisfies certain needs.

In this sense, you very much *do* have a choice as to which role you take on and how well you play it. Family roles are based partly on the perceptions of others, created over the course of a family life. Because of this, you may not be able to change your role in the inheritance drama, even when you don't like it. But, at least to some degree, you can alter how you play it, fine-tuning some of the typical behaviors associated with it.

As you read the various roles below and in the next chapter, think of them as roles that are both partly assigned and partly chosen. The degree to which we consciously choose and play these roles differs for each of us.

The Miserly Type: "It's my money and I don't have to share it with anyone."

Jenna's mother, in her 70s, had accumulated $700,000 in cash, in addition to a home in an affluent suburb of San Francisco. She had inherited and invested the money when her husband died fifteen years earlier. When their father died, Jenna and her brother were in their 40s and had each established their own careers. Neither was looking for a handout. But it was her mother's stinginess that Jenna resented. With more than enough money to take care of herself, Jenna's mother refused to give out more than token gifts of money on her children's birthdays. She was just as miserly with her grandchildren; she claimed to love them dearly and spent time with them, but just couldn't seem to be very generous in giving them gifts.

As Jenna saw it, her mother seemed to get more stingy as she aged. When she tried to talk to her mother about her will and trust and how she wanted her possessions distributed, her mother got angry and told Jenna she was acting like a "vulture in waiting." Jenna repeatedly tried to convince her mother that she only wanted to know her intentions. But her mother refused to discuss her plans. Despite being told by her accountant that it was in her own interest tax-wise to gift $10,000 per year to her children and anyone else she wanted, Jenna's mother could not bring herself to give these gifts.

When I asked Jenna why she thought her mother was so stingy, she told me how her mother had gone through much of her life with no financial security. She was more able to be a loving and giving mother during Jenna's childhood, when there wasn't much to share, but only after Jenna's father died and left everything to Jenna's mother did Jenna see this frightened, stingy, and selfish side of her mom.

Jenna's brother has long ago given up any thought of seeing cash gifts from his mother while she's alive. He accepted that this was the only way she could deal with her insecurity about paying for any help she might need in case of illness. And he was doing well enough that he didn't need any monetary gifts. But his understanding and lack of need didn't keep him from feeling resentful toward his mother, just as Jenna felt. Their resentment made it difficult for them to be as open and loving with their mother as they would have liked to be.

An equally common story is the child who complains that his parent is miserly but gives out periodic "payoffs" to bribe him into doing what the parent wants. The parent may not otherwise feel that the children will do what he wants, so making the gifts of money conditional upon complying with requests becomes the primary tool to get what he wants. It may be to visit the parent or care for him in some way, or to manage his affairs.

Lennie, for example, tells me his father sends him large amounts of money as well as expensive gifts as long as he visits him regularly and does a number of chores for him. These include paying his bills, doing the grocery shopping, and buying him clothes. When Lennie tried to tell his father he doesn't need to keep sending him gifts, that he would be happy to help him because he cares for him, his father simply wouldn't hear of it. He feels that he needs to "insure" that his son will be there to take care of him. In addition, his father likes the feeling of control that goes with this kind of giving.

The Generous Type: "It gives me great pleasure to have you enjoy my money and to pass on some of my possessions to you while I'm still alive."

This type of trustor is happy to see children and grandchildren receive gifts of money and possessions while he or she is alive. These people derive pleasure from helping family members and friends. Relationships with children and extended family are basically positive and nourishing, and the overall principle dictating division of money and possessions is often fairness and equality. Preferences regarding children and situational need are played out subtly. For example, the generous type will quietly write a personal check to an adult child who is in need of financial help to get through a tough time.

I can think of no better example of this type than my own mother, who had always been generous, even before she had much in the way of money or material things to give. She gave of her time and attention throughout her life and found it easy to make others comfortable so that they wanted to share their personal story with her. If anything, at times she was overly generous, giving away what she should have kept for herself and, at times, not asking for what was rightfully hers. Sometimes, this got her in trouble. But most of the time, even if she was being taken advantage of, it simply didn't matter to her. She would say, "The other person needs it more than I do."

Here's an example of what I mean by overly generous: When I reviewed her account records, I noticed she was writing checks ($25 to $50) to extended family members and even family friends for their birthdays. While a few people could have used the money, others were far from needy. The best example was an in-law who was near my mother's age and worth millions of dollars but who was sent a personal check for $50 for her birthday.

For the last few years of her life, my mother gave each of her sons a tax-deductible $10,000 gift. In addition, she gave various other sums to her grandchildren and stepchildren for birthdays and other occasions. She was able to discuss her inheritance plans openly, at least when it came to money, and had prepared a will and trust to handle her estate long before she died. She would ask for and take advice from me regarding her investments.

She was also able to personally give away certain heirlooms and possessions to me, my wife, and my brothers that she wanted us to have. For example, she gave me a beautifully etched silver wine cup that was used for religious services by her grandfather in Russia when he was a rabbi. She explained this history of the cup to me and had me write it down, so that it would not be forgotten.

She gave me art objects, old yearbooks, and framed pictures of her when she was young. And she gave my wife precious jewelry she wanted her to have. It made her feel good to know where these items would be and that they would be cared for. She knew she had enough money to take care of her own needs and was happy to help my brothers and their children as well.

If the generous type of trustor has an ulterior motive of being cared for, visited, or just remembered in a loving way, it is in the background, not something obvious, as it is with the miserly type. Generous trustors are usually people who have spent a lifetime being generous. Being generous with their life savings and personal possessions is simply an extension of this personality trait.

The Martyr Type: "My needs are small— don't worry about me."

This type of trustor lives frugally, acts like she has no assets, and sometimes will share what little she claims she does have freely with others. Some are unable to share with anyone, desiring to amass more money "just to make sure" if anything goes wrong. When she dies, her family discovers significant assets that surprise everyone. Often this person has lived through the Depression or years of poverty or financial reversal. She is unable to overcome the sense of never having enough, fearful of being thrust back into destitution again.

Because of this fear, the martyr type simply can't spend what she has saved. She's never learned to be generous with herself, so family members often reap an unexpected windfall. Sometimes this type will lead a lonely and isolated life and have no heirs. Large amounts of their estate may be left to charitable organizations, religious groups, or social causes. The most interesting of this type is very frugal in spending on herself but is able to give more easily to children or grandchildren.

For example, Sylvia, 74, lived in an unassuming small house in the

Midwest. She worked her whole life as a librarian and enjoyed charity work with her church. She liked giving her teenage grandchildren generous gifts of money and buying them clothes when they came to visit. But the children could not understand how their grandmother could afford to be so generous with them when they saw how modest her home was and how little she indulged herself in any sort of luxury. She would often say to them, "Don't worry about me—I have more than enough for myself," even though it appeared that she had very little in the way of comforts.

When she died, her family discovered that she had somehow been able to save over a million dollars in cash, CDs, and bonds that had been accumulating interest for over thirty years. She was so secretive about these savings that not even her children had any idea she had anything like that kind of money.

While she left her children and grandchildren a portion of her inheritance, the greater bulk of it was left to her favorite church, where she had spent over fifteen years volunteering her services in a thrift shop connected to the church—and where she had gotten most of her own clothes.

The Controlling/Punishing Type: "If you want to see your inheritance, you better do what I say."

This is one of the more difficult trustor types and common enough that we will go into much more detail about it in Chapter 4. For now, we just want to identify this type by saying that much of how one generation controls the behavior of their offspring and even the following generation (their grandchildren) can be typified, at least to some degree, by a controlling-punishing relationship. Nowhere is this more clear than in the control exerted through the threat of disinheritance.

Some adult children live their whole lives with the threat of disinheritance in the background, coloring much of their decision making when it comes to whether or not they follow the dictates of their parents. And, of course, the more wealthy the parents and the more luxurious the lifestyle, the more powerful is this threatening sword they wield. In some very wealthy families, the threat of disinheritance is the main theme running through family relationships—a more powerful motivator than love, blood affiliation, or social status.

Many movies, plays, novels, and television shows have been based on one rendition of this theme: the resentful child who conforms to or rebels against the wishes of the wealthy parents, always knowing in the back of his mind that a longed-for inheritance is the bargaining chip that the parents will play.

The controlling parent gives to the child when the child does what the parent demands. By the time the child has become an adult, he has learned well how it works. In the short term, the parent rewards the adult child by giving money, gifts, and various other "payoffs" to ensure obedience to the parent's wishes. More overriding pressure is felt by the child as the aging parent increases his focus on the topic of inheritance and how easily it may be withheld.

This trustor type is often ruthless in his willingness to directly threaten the child with disinheritance, for example: "If you don't live close to me, I will write you out of my will." But the threat may also come indirectly, in more of an implied fashion, like this: "If you accompany me on the cruise, I will pay for your passage." It is implied that if the child doesn't go with the parent, the disinheritance threat is always looming.

You may be asking, "How is it implied?" It is implied because the child has learned over a lifetime that score is being kept for *all* of her behavior, and the life of promise to be afforded through the inheritance is always on the line. It doesn't even need to be said directly. But more cruel and punishing parents make sure they say it directly and say it often. And they are not shy about making the adult child feel as needy as possible. At worst, this results in her believing she may be unable to survive without the inheritance.

Some focus more heavily on punishing than controlling. For example, a generous birthday gift that the child has learned to expect from the parent may be "downgraded" to a less expensive gift as a way to say, "All is not right with us—I'm still feeling resentment." There are many forms of parental punishing, some of which we will identify in other chapters.

The Wishful Thinker: "Don't worry about it, everything will be just fine."

This type leads his spouse and children to believe he has made provisions, such as a will, life insurance, and savings, to take care of them when he dies. But he puts off drawing up a will and has no savings to speak of. He is hopeful of being able to provide but in fact has no plan or means to carry out his wishful thinking. He wants his family not to worry but doesn't think about the bitter disappointment they will have to endure when they learn the truth of his financial condition.

Men play this role predominantly but not exclusively. Some may purposefully lie and deceive to paint a more positive picture of their assets than is justified. When they die, this deception leads to family surprise, anger, and disappointment. Family members feel abandoned, as they had been led to believe the parent had something to transfer. No such luck.

Other wishful thinkers are not so much deceitful as they are simply poor managers and sloppy planners. They may not earn enough to save much for retirement, let alone any kind of inheritance. They hope that things will change. But this hope is never made concrete through action.

It requires a moderately naive partner and children to make this role of wishful thinker effective. If a spouse or other family member knows the true financial situation of the wishful thinker, he will be confronted when he tries to tell them that "everything will be fine." It is because communication may be strained or may break down altogether when it comes to estate planning that the wishful thinker is, at times, able to be convincing. When a spouse and children don't ask enough questions and demand proof of answers, the wishful thinker may placate them with what they want to hear to help cope with the uneasy situation. Again, the more the wishful thinker is able to convince his family they will be provided for, the more disappointed they will be when they learn the truth upon his death.

This disappointment represents about as pure an example of the old adage of "adding insult to injury" as you might find. Not only are family members left the emotional injury of losing a parent, they're shocked with the insult that he died having been deceptive about his estate and has left them little or nothing.

Reggie had never much cared about making a lot of money. He got by in his work as a skilled electrician well enough to pay his mortgage on a modest home and to raise his daughter. In his 60s, he had a heart attack that put him out of work and into retirement. Although he would tell his wife not to worry, that she would be taken care of, she could never pin him down as to how she was to survive financially when he died.

The heart attack had shocked her into the realization that Reggie had little savings put away and just a small life insurance policy that had been the result of his union affiliation. She herself had worked for many years as a nurse in a hospital. But her benefits were limited and she had wanted to believe that her husband had been thinking of her survival when he died.

He had, in fact, been *thinking* about it—but only in a wishful way. His life insurance policy wouldn't go very far. He simply wasn't able to build up any savings over the years, choosing instead to spend money that didn't go to expenses on his hobby of electric trains. His wife knew how much he loved his hobby and wouldn't place any limits on his spending when it came to buying trains and related items. But his short-coming was not being able to be honest with her about how little he had been able to save, instead always telling her what she wanted to hear: "Don't worry, dear, everything will be all right."

Had it not been for the fact that their one daughter was making a good living as an attorney, Reggie's wife would not have been able to manage on what was left her when a few years later he died from his second heart attack. In fact, it was because of her guilt over feeling so angry about his leaving her with no inheritance that she had come to see me. She came to realize that it was partly due to her own unwilling-ness to be more confrontational with Reggie that she ended up in this predicament.

The Squandering Type: "I'm spending my children's inheritance. Live for the moment, baby, know what I mean?"
This type spends much or all of what they could pass on to their children on pleasures: lavish vacations, fine dining, fancy cars, expensive clothes, plush furniture, social and athletic club memberships, the latest appliances, etc. He or she may be in a second marriage and want to impress and please the new partner. Or he may simply be indulging himself in an attempt to make up for what was not permissible earlier in life or was kept in check by a previous partner. This type tends to adopt a philosophy that discourages any obligation to children and promotes enjoying the fruits of a lifetime of labor.

There are at least two main varieties of the squandering type. One is what we might call a *perpetual* squanderer. The spending of their children's would-be inheritance is consistent with a personality that tends to be poor with money management. They tend to have a "here-today-gone-tomorrow" attitude about spending and often appear to be comfortable with living on the financial edge. Often these people have shown a long-term pattern of quickly spending any money they have earned or been gifted, with no ability to delay gratification of desires or save money for the future. They do not just spend freely what they have, they spend wastefully.

The adult children of the squandering type have—after a lifetime of watching the parent's inability to manage money responsibly—come to expect little in the way of any monetary inheritance. What inheritance they do receive may come in the form of possessions that the parent has collected along the way in their extravagant bursts of spending and accumulating. But they may also find themselves having to take care of unpaid debts that the impulsive parent has left behind.

Because baby boomers have grown up expecting to have what they want when they want it, I predict that a special variety (perhaps we should call it "Squanderer Lite") of this type will become a more common inheritance personality to be reckoned with over the next decade or two. This variety will be boomers who do not so much squander their money as consciously choose to spend their savings largely on themselves rather than earmark it for inheritance. We will come back to the impact of this "spend it while you're alive" thinking on the behavior of baby boomers in Chapter 6.

The second variety of the squandering type, closer to the thinking of the boomers mentioned above, acquires the mentality much later in life. This *nouveau squanderer* type is more likely to be in their 60s or 70s when the behavior begins to surface, rather than in their 40s or 50s, or rather than spending over a whole lifetime. Often they have shown a careful and conscientious approach to finances leading up to the time of a crucial event. It is only when there is a sudden, shocking, and usually catastrophic event that they change their thinking about how they want to live the rest of their lives and deal with their money.

For example, one person I worked with, in his early 60s, had carefully built up a healthy savings account throughout his life. That amount was easily enough to take him through the rest of his expected life span and afford him a relaxed and worry-free retirement. He paid his bills in a timely manner, managed credit carefully, and prided himself on handling his finances responsibly.

He had two adult children and had always felt he had an obligation to leave them some of what he had worked so hard to obtain. But when his wife died of a short and sudden illness, his whole philosophy of life changed. He realized that he could no longer take living a long life for granted and that an illness or accident could end his life at any time. The terrorist events of September 11, 2001, and the ensuing insecurity only reinforced this thinking.

Furthermore, he wanted to give himself some of the material things and pleasures that he had denied himself for most of his life. When he came to see me, he wanted me to help him change his thinking without feeling guilty.

For some, the penetrating realization—from the death of a spouse, a serious accident, or a personal near-death experience—that they won't live forever might make them insure themselves more heavily and think about how they want to make sure all provisions for their will are up to date. It might even lead them to add to their savings accounts or begin to give monetary gifts to their children. But that's not what happened with my patient.

The sudden death of his wife made him realize how little he had allowed himself to travel and do some of the other things he wanted to do. He had always hoped to do these things with his wife, and now realized that would never be possible. So he did what he believed was the next best thing. He didn't wait long before beginning the dating process and, within a few months, found a woman he felt compatible with and wanted to marry. And he began spending his savings much more freely, to the point that his children began to wonder whether he was thinking clearly. He tried to tell them how his philosophy of life had changed since the death of their mother, but his children didn't believe him.

Why? Because they thought it had to be the influence of his new wife, who they weren't all that crazy about. He began committing large amounts to travel and new clothes. He also began investing in the stock market when it was into the second year of its bear market. While my patient would argue that he wasn't really squandering his savings, the fact that his free spending was so counter to his previous conservative habits sure made it appear that way to his children.

Seeing their father spend so freely was scary enough. But hearing him talk about his new philosophy of *carpe diem* or "seize the day," reinforced their fear that he wasn't concerned about protecting his savings—their inheritance.

The fact that he wanted my help to feel less guilty about his decision allowed us the chance to help structure his new lifestyle in a way that would ensure the preservation of a portion of his savings. Once he was able to show his family that he could both spend more freely and protect his future, his children became more accepting of his decision to "live a little."

The issue with the noveau squanderer is their change of lifestyle. There will always be a segment of conservative types who are shocked into wanting to change their careful habits. For them, this equals living more spontaneously and more fully. And that means spending more money on themselves.

If they can afford to spend some of their savings and don't get too carried away, as my patient was able to do, their family may view this as a positive change—even a breaking through of rigid habits that have constricted the parent's ability to live more in the present rather than always thinking about the future. Then it need not be viewed as squandering their money. For those who go too far, however, and end up regretting not having enough to take them through the rest of their lives, the change in lifestyle may indeed be seen as wasteful—both in their own eyes and in the eyes of their children.

CHAPTER 3
ROLES IN THE FAMILY DRAMA:
RECEIVERS

We now turn our attention to all those on the other end of the inheritance equation: the beneficiaries, or receivers. See which type best describes your role in your family.

The Wicked One: "You'll get yours, my little pretty! All in good time . . ."

An estranged or bitter sibling, an aunt or uncle, a mother-in-law, stepmother, or any other person who appears to need to turn an already difficult emotional situation into a torturous ordeal may be playing this role.

One defining characteristic of the wicked one is that their actions, from the point of view of other family members and outsiders, appear *not* to be the result of ignorance or self-protection. The distasteful behavior has the look and feel of someone intentionally trying to be hurtful or cruel by taking advantage of the vulnerability of other family members.

The wicked one may be doing something that is, for her, generally consistent with her personality and how she typically behaves with others. Or she may purposely adopt (or become unconsciously ensnared in) the role specifically to address feelings of greediness when money and possessions are on the line. In any case, the wicked one becomes an extremely difficult person to cope with when an inheritance is being divided. This is intriguing to watch from a distance but not someone you want to be negotiating with directly, because those who play this role only want to make a bad situation worse.

The wicked one may do everything possible to turn family members against one another. They accomplish this through gossip, lies, innuendo, backstabbing, focusing on petty issues, and not cooperating. Threats of legal battles are often part of their arsenal. So are attempts to play siblings against one another. When their threats don't succeed in getting what they want, they may initiate lengthy legal entanglements. She may strike at any time—before or during a crisis—or may come out of the woodwork only after a family death has occurred.

The objective of the wicked one is to get his share of the inheritance without regard for what damage he does to relationships or the future of the family unit in general. This person exploits the situation to play out long-term resentments now that the parent is gone, and therefore unable to moderate between siblings and the rest of the family. This is why there is a hurtful quality to his actions. It's not just wanting to get his share *but also to get back* at those he believes have harmed him along the way.

The wicked one doesn't care that estate money will be wasted paying for legal fees and various other costs. He will use whatever techniques are available to further his goal of taking no prisoners and creating as much havoc as possible. What he wants is to make others miserable, along with getting what he believes is his share of an inheritance.

In-laws, stepparents, and stepchildren are likely players in this role, as they may perceive themselves as being on the "outside looking in" and less concerned about the ongoing coherence of the core family unit. The wicked one may be viewed by other family members as instigating confusion, disagreements, and ill will between family members.

Because of the heightened sensitivity to—and more penetrating impact of—emotion during the inheritance process, the ones who choose to play this role are unforgettable. Long after financial estate matters come to a close, other family members will talk about and scorn the wicked one. They may even be subject to lengthy or permanent abandonment. You do *not* want to play this part in your family! But here's someone who did.

Ronnie, 35, had always been angry and resentful that his sisters were closer to their father than he was. He never got the attention from his father that they did and was never shown the approval he was looking for. While his father was alive, Ronnie's resentment had taken the form of skipping out on a number of family celebrations, usually with some kind of lame last-minute excuse. When he did manage to attend family occasions, he would drink too much and end up saying something to upset one of his sisters or his parents.

Ronnie's mother felt sorry for him, knowing that his father truly *wasn't* as fond of him as he was of his daughters. She tried to make up for what he didn't get from his father by giving him small gifts, calling him frequently, and even paying for some of his schemes when he tried something new to help himself. But Ronnie was never able to sit down and discuss his resentments directly with his father. So when his father died, Ronnie went on a drinking binge that lasted for two weeks. And then he decided to make life a living hell for his sisters and his mother by hiring an attorney to block a smooth settling of the estate.

Although his mother received most of his father's money and possessions, the father had had a trust drawn up that provided for his daughters to receive a share of the money immediately. Because Ronnie had not been included this allowance, he felt he had to fight to get what he thought was fair—to be given the same immediate money that his sisters received.

The torture included frequent harassing calls to both of his sisters, threats that he would do damage to their homes if he wasn't included in the inheritance, and a bombardment of e-mails to both of them that were demeaning, foulmouthed, and intimidating.

Even his mother could no longer make excuses for him and pleaded with him to back off and let the estate be settled peacefully. But his anger and resentment toward his father was so intense that he did not care what his mother wanted, despite the fact that he knew how hard it was for her to cope with the loss of her lifelong partner.

Because of his threats to his sisters and the fact that he'd assaulted his girlfriend during one of his binges, the family ended up having a restraining order issued just to keep him at bay. In the end, he was unsuccessful at getting any part of his father's inheritance. But he was quite successful at harassing his family while they were trying to grieve the loss of their father.

The Favorite Child: "Mom loves me the most, you'll see."

This role is perhaps the most coveted of all the roles that siblings like to play. The important thing to remember about this part in the family drama is that it is defined by what the child *believes* is his relationship to the parent—which is not necessarily how the parent actually feels. Sometimes the child is in fact correct—the parent's behavior indicates favoritism toward the child. This, however, doesn't mean the parent will admit to favoritism to the other children, even when it may appear obvious to everyone. Other times, feeling favored is simply what the child *wishes* to believe, as it makes him feel special in relation to the parent and superior in relation to siblings.

In some families, multiple siblings believe they are favored; they may either secretly hold this belief or broadcast it to all other family members. This is not all that uncommon. It is actually a sign of a relatively healthy family, since the parents have managed to create the feeling in each child that he or she is the favored one.

The common and "politically correct" role for parents is to typically downplay favoritism among their children. Sensitive and caring parents do not want to blatantly express preference toward any one child because it is not what they believe a good parent should feel. Not only do they like the idea of loving each child equally, but they also like to believe each child is being treated fairly in relation to the others.

While this is a nice idea, the reality is that when parents are honest with themselves, they know that each child has a different relationship to them. And some children are simply going to create a closer, more loving relationship than others, especially over the long haul of a lifetime together. Parents should admit their own biases *to themselves* rather than pretend that each child is loved equally. Why? Because in admitting their preferences, they are then in a better position to consciously and honestly decide how they want to compensate for those biases in the way they behave toward the children.

When it comes to inheritance, being favored in no way means that one child will necessarily receive a larger share of the inheritance pie from a parent's will or trust. Since most parents are not anxious to create wars among their adult children, it is usually only when one child has been disowned or disfavored to the extreme that children will not receive equal inheritance with regard to money.

Anytime a parent expresses a clear preference for one child receiving more than another, it is a surefire prescription for sibling resentment. Most parents can figure this out. So it's only when their own strong emotions take over—or when there are extraordinary circumstances that dictate favoritism—that they indulge in clearly favoring one over the other.

But that doesn't mean favoritism won't be shown indirectly, through various gifts and favors while the parent is alive. And there is a good case to be made that this is the best way to deal with parental preference, rather than have it be played out through the more formal and legal inheritance process.

The favorite child often gains this status through having developed a more intimate relationship with the parent over a lifetime. This may be from time spent together, a greater willingness to take care of the parent when needed, or special circumstances in childhood that made for a tighter bonding between parent and child.

For example, medical problems that needed attention, such as a childhood disease or handicap that required ongoing parental nursing care, intensifies the parent–child relationship. A major accident or illness that threatens the child's life may stimulate the special feeling by the parent, as they are faced with possible loss of the child. In some families, where the child happened to fall in the birth order may create the special bonding.

The favorite child—if it is clear to siblings that he or she *is* the favorite—tends to broadcast, either subtly or directly, this fact to sibs and other family members. Equally problematic is when the parent voices that favoritism to the other sibs. More often, the favoritism is not so much voiced as it is simply demonstrated. Behind-the-back gifts of money and possessions show the favorite how much he or she means to the parent and fortify the sense of specialness of the child.

One of the issues that can make this role difficult for sibs of the favored one is the knowledge that with this favored position go the rewards of this status. Sibs typically resent this special treatment, especially when it is displayed in an obvious way to the rest of the family. Since these resentments have been created over a lifetime, they are easily brought to the surface when inheritance issues must be faced.

The Lost and Forgotten Child: "Don't forget, she's my mom, too."

In some families, a child, grandchild, or stepchild may "come out of the woodwork" just before or after the parent dies, despite not having been seen or heard from for years and thus not having been considered an integral part of the family. The child may be estranged from the family or born out of wedlock to the parent or one of the adult children.

For example, a grandchild born out of wedlock may suddenly make a legal claim for inheritance even though the parent has specifically excluded him from the will. But the child sees a possible chance to get money or possessions that are not rightfully his, yet legally debatable, and decides it's worth going after simply because it's there. This, of course, is more likely to happen when the child feels bitterness toward other family members and doesn't stand to lose much in making a claim against the estate. Decisions made like this are usually poorly thought out and regretted when the short-term possible gain later does not seem worth the long-term degeneration of family relationships.

Like the wicked one, the lost and forgotten child already feels so alienated that he doesn't perceive much risk in upsetting other family members. If this child is the biological offspring of the parent, he may have legal rights that can create problems for other siblings, especially if the parent has not had the foresight to have a will with specific instructions as to how he wants this child to be considered.

Remember that no matter how careful a parent has been in estate planning, anyone can challenge the will at any time—whether or not they have good reason to. In identifying the various roles those on the receiving end play, my purpose is simply to help you become aware of all the potential parts that may make themselves felt in the inheritance process.

The Problem Child: "I've got the most problems and need the most help, so don't begrudge me getting more than you do."

Now we come to perhaps the most common (but not most highly regarded) role that someone may play in the inheritance drama. This is the one "character" that inspires so many plotlines for movies and novels. The problem child tends to engender resentment among sibs, since her position is so vulnerable and susceptible to other family members' attacks.

The problem child needs the greatest attention in the family—not for his abilities and accomplishments but for his weaknesses and blunders. This child demands more time and effort from parents to be bailed out of his problems. Depending on their tolerance, parents either resent the attention demanded by the problem child or, when reaching the point of emotional and financial exhaustion, throw up their hands in despair and give up.

The dynamic developed between parents and the problem child can be an interesting one, since one parent may become the rejecting, punitive one while the other balances this role by being more accepting, forgiving, and supportive. Typically the father is more rejecting and the mother more accepting, but sometimes the roles are reversed. The problem child may have had good reason in early life to end up playing this part. Either because of a severe illness, handicap, or just personality differences, he ends up being unable to accomplish at the same level as other sibs.

But this part is not just about accomplishment or the lack of it. Far more draining is the perpetual effort parents and, sometimes, others in the family put into helping the child simply get by in life with the minimum amount of chaos. The problems this child creates may exhaust family members both financially and emotionally, because often these people do not seem to learn from their past experiences. Instead, they tend to repeat the behaviors that get them in trouble.

For our purposes, what is important to remember is that this role can end up being a powerful one—particularly because of the goods and services the problem child can procure from parents and the outside world. While the problem child usually really does have problems, he often displays his weakness manipulatively, hoping to gain favor out of the sympathy that it may generate in others. This manipulation is often, but not always, intentional.

Bad debts, bad marriages, impulsive decisions, the inability to hold jobs, problems with substance abuse or the law—these and more are what the problem child presents to the family for help. All it requires is one sympathetic parent who is willing to try and bail him out by repeatedly throwing money and attention at him for the child to learn that this role has its rewards.

The psychological dynamic operating here is basically that if a child cannot get attention by doing well, he will get it by doing poorly. As long as the child receives the desired attention and help from the parents, he is not concerned with what means he uses to get it.

In the self-help literature of the late eighties and nineties, trying to help the problem child by giving him what he thinks he needs was called *enabling*. The parent or other family member would feel sorry for the child and pay the money or perform the behavior asked to help temporarily relieve him of his predicament. The problem, however, was exacerbated when it became evident that giving the person what he thought he needed only taught him that he did not have to change his thinking or behavior—he only needed to learn how to get others to solve his problems for him.

The child was "enabled" by the parent to keep doing the same old behavior because he would be bailed out. There was no good reason for the child to stop the toxic behavior or to be faced with the consequences of his actions if someone was always coming to his rescue.

When it comes to inheritance, the problem child expects that the death of the parent means a surviving parent or sibling will "come to the rescue" and continue to play the same enabling role as the deceased parent once did. Additionally, he has a sense of entitlement that survivors ought to give him a larger piece of the estate pie simply because he's more needy than they are. The motto for this role might be "He who screws up most, wins." That is, if others are feeling sorry for him and willing to play the enabling role.

The Trust Fund Child: "If I don't suck up, he'll deny me my money."

This role is an exclusive one. You can't just take it on. It's one that you step into by virtue of being in a wealthy family. Further, the family has to have set up a trust fund (or at least intimated that large amounts of money are available) that the child is made aware of early in life. The parents make it clear that the child will be well taken care of "someday," and that all she has to do is be the child her parents want her to be to earn the riches and privileges promised. Sometimes receiving some money from the trust fund is dependent on the child reaching a certain age, when the parents believe the child will be mature enough to handle the money responsibly. Then the child will receive a bigger portion after the death of one or both parents.

While being a trust fund child has its obvious material advantages, I have witnessed the consequences of the stress it puts adolescents and adults under when they feel they must always be concerned with whether or not their actions are gaining parental approval. They end up in my consulting office, dealing with a childhood of forced behavior compliance. They feel anger and resentment for how money, comfort, and security have been used to shape their choices.

Parents are more effective in producing compliant children if they have been consistently generous with them throughout the children's lives. Trust fund children are shown how wonderful a life of luxury may be and begin to believe they could never live without it. Once they've tasted how much easier life can be when they materially have everything that money can offer, some will do most anything not to lose this advantage.

Like all the inheritance roles, however, there are complications. Some rich kids like to get into trouble, and hope their parents' wealth and privilege will bail them out. They become problem children, except they have the advantage of having parents who can easily afford to indulge them, as long as they are willing. I have also seen how the trust fund child may decide not to make much effort to accomplish anything in the world, becoming complacent and indulging in trivial pursuits that are not fulfilling or meaningful.

Unable to overcome having everything handed to them, some trust fund children lose motivation to expand their personal boundaries or challenge themselves. The trust fund child who is content to live off his parents' wealth and social standing and never really accomplishes anything on his own is a well-known stereotype.

Generations ago there was more respect for the "genteel" man or woman who didn't dirty his or her hands with common work or concerns about money; today we don't have much respect for those who indulge in playing this part, especially if they aren't contributing in some way to the betterment of others and not just obsessed with themselves and their personal pleasures. But this doesn't mean that others don't secretly envy the material comforts of these people, whether or not what they have has been personally earned.

The trust fund child who wishes to live off his parents' good fortune feels no need to strive in the frantic and competitive worlds of academics, business, the arts, charities, or anything else. The trust fund child thinks, "If my parents have already reached the top, why not stand on their shoulders and enjoy the view? Why strive when I have all the money and possessions I will ever need if I just play my cards right?"

These people will tell you that travel, shopping, hobbies, and accumulating bigger and better luxuries is a full-time job, if you pursue it seriously. Not surprisingly, some view striving as being for "jerks" or "working stiffs" who aren't as fortunate as they are to have everything handed to them on a silver trust fund platter. And they really don't care whether or not you approve of their thinking.

The Adopted Child: "I brought so much joy to your life when you couldn't have children. Please do right by me in return."

The adopted child role is a shoo-in not to have inheritance problems if she is the only child of the trustor parent and the relationship has been a strong one. This role gets interesting only when there are biological offspring of the parent in the picture. The adopted child expects to be given equal treatment by the trustor parent as that of her siblings, and trouble starts if she isn't accorded this standing.

Biological children, if they aren't too greedy and have a good relationship with the adopted sibling, may be very accepting of the adopted children receiving equal benefits, if that is what the parent wishes. But it is possible for the sense of specialness that comes with the biological connection to surface and for this to lead to resentment if the adopted child is given equal inheritance status.

It also becomes problematic if the parent decides not to leave an equal share to the adopted and biological children. The adopted child may contest the will, believing she has every right to a fair share. This may also occur if the child is not legally adopted but a more distant relative or family friend who becomes close enough to be *considered* "adopted."

The Child Who Has His Own: "Don't deny me just because I'm smart, successful, and never needed your money to bail me out."

The eldest child in a family often—but not exclusively—plays this role. The child has sometimes been the "pride and joy" of the parents, accomplishing everything the parents wanted for her and hoped for her sibs. She has learned to support herself financially and has not needed assistance along the way. Those playing this role tend to be stable, conforming, and adjusted to career choices, and have established a level of comfort, root-edness, and involvement in their communities. They often balance out the designated problem child in a family, who, much to his dismay, is often compared to "the one who has his own."

Those who "have their own" are proud of their accomplishments and like the fact they haven't needed parental financial support, even though they continue to need their emotional support. The inheritance issue that may arise for this child is how the success she has enjoyed will influence the thinking of the trustor parent when it comes to division of money and possessions. Because the child playing this role has made the parent proud, communication between them is usually good. But having good communication doesn't mean it's easy to ask about inheri-tance plans, because that means facing the taboo.

Parents may take for granted the years of accomplishment and sta-bility this child has demonstrated. And when it comes time for inheri-tance consideration, it is exactly this long-term success that may end up backfiring for the "one who has his own." This child may be left less in the will since parents may believe he doesn't need the same financial as-sistance as other sibs who have not been as skilled or fortunate.

The "has his own" child sees the other sibs who are having a tougher time financially receiving money, furniture, and generous gifts of various kinds. She notices that the needy sibs are given five times the amount she is for a birthday or holiday gift. She feels resentment that her success means she may not be given the same inheritance consideration from her parents.

Because this theme touches on the core issue of equality and fairness among children—regardless of their success—this child may come to believe things are backward. In other words, she who does the best and makes her parents most proud receives the least when it comes to parental handouts. This will probably create conflict while the parent is alive. But it definitely becomes more problematic among sibs when the parent dies if equal shares of money and possessions are not given to all.

While the adult child who has been able to create a stable financial footing in her life enjoys her independence and sense of accomplishment, a nagging thought remains that sibs who are not so successful will actually benefit more from the parent's generosity and desire to help the sibs who are most needy. The issue here is not one of *need*, but of *equality* from the view of the "child who has his own."

From both the trustor parent and needy child's point of view, the issue, of course, is need, *not* equality. They think, "Why shouldn't the one who needs help the most receive it?" They believe that the fact that one or more children are doing fine on their own and don't require assistance only makes it more fitting that the parent help the one who hasn't done as well. The basic conflict of need versus equality between sibs, in terms of treatment by parents, is played out both during the lifetime of the trustor and after he or she dies.

Later, we will come back to some of the ways this conflict of need versus equality is played out. For now, it need only be added that the role of the "one who has her own" requires a willingness to understand that what may be considered *fair* (some need more than others) is not always going to be seen as *equal* (everyone should receive the same, regardless of need). And whether or not things turn out to be equal, how much of an issue to make must be carefully considered in the context of the total relationship with siblings. The final thing to remember is that—like many other issues that become emotionally loaded when a parent dies—a whole lifetime of evaluation of where one stands in relation to sibs in a family is being played out, not just what may be fair or equal.

The Second Wife/Husband: "I'm the one who loves you now. Please be sure to provide for me. After all, you promised me you would."

Second (or more) marriage situations become problematic when the relationship between the stepmother or stepfather and the biological children of the person he or she marries is either weak to begin with or deteriorates over time. The children come to believe that the stepparent is scheming to deprive them of part or all of their rightful inheritance. Even if the stepparent is not actively scheming to take something away, his or her very existence may become potentially threatening when it comes to inheritance. Because of this, the second wife/husband role is one of the prime ones to end up being transformed into a "wicked" or "evil" role.

In other words, when the biological children of the parent resent the stepparent, they may over time come to view him as "evil" because they believe this person is intent on taking inheritance money or possessions from them. This is more likely to occur if the stepparent is much younger than the person she marries or comes into the parent's life toward the end. The labeling of a stepparent as "evil" is also more likely if the biological children simply don't like or trust his or her motives. Basically, the children will look for any reason to deny the stepparent what the parent wants her to have simply because it diminishes their own share of the financial pie. So, the stepparent is going to have a tough time being accepted and appreciated unless this person goes out of her way to ingratiate herself to her spouse's children. One reason for this is that adult children are not quick to accept another person coming into the life of their surviving or divorced parent.

Of course, if the stepparent seems interested in lavishly spending the parent's money while he is alive, this gives the children reason to be concerned and adds fuel to the fire of distrust. Stepparents are always, in the eyes of the children, a "step" away from having the same rights as them. And the children don't often let this escape their awareness, especially when inheritance issues come into play.

Adult children on both sides of the equation—the parent's and the biological children of the stepparent—may actively solicit preference from their respective parent if they do not already feel that the parent is taking them and their needs into full consideration.

> **！** Money and possessions tend to cut to the quick of family alliances, especially blood relationships. Even after long-term second marriages of fifteen to twenty-five years or more, when it comes time for inheritance to be dealt with, adult children want to make sure they are being considered and provided for—and most are not going to lose any sleep if their share is larger because the stepparent's share is smaller.

For example, in a second and lasting marriage for both, Sam had been with Millie for twenty-three years. When he died, everything they had accumulated together was Millie's to do with what she pleased. But Millie knew that certain items were Sam's, even though he'd bought them after they had married. Although they were not all that valuable monetarily, Sam made a point of specifically stating in his will that he wanted them to go to his own children by his first marriage. The items included a desk, bookshelf, file cabinet, and old computer. Millie only used the desk sparingly. Because she knew it was Sam's, she never let herself really rearrange the items in the desk and make it her own.

When Millie died, as prescribed by Sam's will, the items went to Sam's children. This is an example of the emotional value that items of relatively little monetary value may hold for one's children and grandchildren. It's also an example of how certain items never really transfer ownership to the second wife or husband, no matter how long they may be together. Even though Millie got to use the items after Sam died, she never really felt they were hers. His children made it clear to Millie's children when she died: What was *once* his was *always* his.

The Teacher-Guru: "I'm the one who supported and coached you. A small gift of your appreciation surely isn't too much to ask."

Someone outside the family who has been involved with the trustor as an important person may join the cast. It may be as a spiritual teacher, financial adviser, health-care professional, psychotherapist, or any other role in which a person can gain the confidence of the trustor and help her deal with the emotional, practical, financial, or spiritual affairs of life.

Those who take on this role toward the end of the trustor's life, playing a key part in their care and maintenance, are more prone to see themselves as being so indispensable and deserving as to be remembered when it comes time for inheritance gifts. Believing that one is deserving of being put in a will versus simply being paid for one's services—no matter how vital the service or how kind the caregiver—may be based on greed and an inflated sense of self-importance.

It may, of course, simply be an attempt to take advantage of the situation. One of the reasons helpers become so vital is due to the vulnerable position that some older trustors are in at this time in their lives. Those who are basically living on their own are more likely to become ensnared in this kind of relationship. With medical, financial, emotional, and spiritual issues to deal with, they may easily become overly dependent on the people around them. Because of this vulnerability, the trustor may make promises to "take care of" the helper in the will so that he or she is not abandoned in a time of need.

This is more likely to occur if the helping relationship has been developed over a few years and the helper has come to be a good friend to the trustor, in addition to the helping role. When an aging parent has no family members looking after her to monitor exploitive relationships, neediness may overcome clear thinking and good judgment.

While you might think that adult children do their best to prevent a teacher or helper from being included in a will, this kind of thing happens more than it should. Many older people have no family to care for them when they need it, as they are dealing with issues of physical deterioration, illness, death, and dying. They may believe that even when they do have family to help them, the teacher-helper is showing a greater interest, devoting more time, and being of more assistance than family members. What may happen is that the emotional and psychological vulnerability of the trustor makes him confuse the service provider role with friendship. Of course, some of these teachers and providers do in fact become close enough to the trustor over time to be considered good friends. The situation is, unfortunately, ripe for exploitation if no one is carefully watching over the trustor to protect him from being taken advantage of.

This role is worth including because even a small share being given to a person playing this part is likely to be resented by family members, who may believe the helper has in some way manipulated their parent to include them in their will. There have been a number of court cases, for example, that have contested the undue influence believed to be

exerted by a psychotherapist or spiritual teacher on the inheritance thinking and actions of a trustor.

The Best Friend and Confidant: "We go way back—don't forget it."

Much like the teacher-guru but even more so, the best friend and confidant role is most likely to be abused when family members are nonexistent or the friend has created a dependent relationship with the trustor.
Single trustors without children may be so appreciative of a longtime
friend who is willing to help care for them that they wish to leave an inheritance gift to them. There is no problem with this role unless there
are family members in the picture who don't understand why a friend of
their parent should receive any monetary gift.

They are more understanding of the friend receiving a treasured
personal possession that both may have shared in some way. This is by
far the most common way that a friend may be involved in inheritance.
In addition, as with children, the trustor may simply give the friend a gift
of money or a possession while alive, so that no potential problems with
family members are created.

A true good friend expects nothing in the way of inheritance. But a
trustor who wants to reward a friend for being loyal over many years or
even a lifetime may view a gift of money as a way to do it, especially if
that friend needs it. When the close friend has been promised money or
a possession of value but ends up not being written into the will, it is possible the friend may make a claim against the estate, believing she has
been unfairly omitted because she was "promised" something by the
trustor.

For example, Marge had been June's close friend for over twenty-
five years. June had one son who lived far away from her. She came to
depend on the kindness of Marge to help with daily tasks that became
more than she could handle by herself as her eyesight and arthritis wors-
ened. June had been living off the interest from the trust her husband
had set up for her many years before he died.

June felt that without Marge's help she would have had to hire someone to drive her to the market and various other appointments. So she would periodically tell Marge that she would leave her something when she died. In the beginning, they would laugh about it. But, over the years, Marge came to expect she would be included in June's will. While June would periodically treat her friend to lunch, she would not hand her money directly, nor did Marge ever ask for any compensation for her kindness.

As is often the case with these kinds of promises, June never actually had her friend written into her will. What little she had to give in the way of money and possessions was left to her son and a church. Marge felt some disappointment and even considered making a claim against the estate, but was talked out of this by an attorney who made it clear that without any written agreement between the two, June's verbal promise meant nothing.

The Daddy-Doll Girlfriend: "I brought you so much pleasure and made you feel young again! Take care of me good, Sugar Daddy."

This role is perhaps best typified in the extreme by a young Anna Nicole Smith marrying a billionaire in his 80s shortly before his death, then fighting and winning in court against his son to get her promised share of his fortune. A younger woman marries a significantly older man or a young man marries a significantly older woman, ostensibly for love and companionship but with money in mind. It's a rather popular and intriguing coupling in the social world in its various forms.

The role becomes problematic when family members object to the marriage, believing their parent is being taken advantage of by a far younger partner. Because it tends to scream out exploitation, the "daddy-doll" relationship is trouble enough, even when unrelated to inheritance. But it becomes toxic to a family when the parent dies and the "doll" has been left a significant share of money. Even when the "doll" is given only a portion, it is reasonable when adult children and other family members object to the arrangement and do their best to have the younger spouse legally removed from financial consideration and gain.

One interesting thing about this relationship is that often both people are quite aware and open about the fact that they are exchanging youth, beauty, companionship, and sex for money, material comfort, and lifestyle. The age gap between the two obviously need not be as extreme as it was with Smith and her sugar daddy. A gap of anywhere from fifteen to twenty years is enough for it to be viewed as a daddy-doll entanglement.

Of course, the couple need not necessarily end up married. In fact, this type of inheritance role is more often played out as an ongoing affair that an older and married man or (less often) woman is having with a younger "friend." Because the younger person may be "kept" financially by the older one, often there is a direct or implied promise of some kind of inheritance when the older one dies, assuming the relationship lasts a specified period of time.

When someone who the trustor financially supported plays the role, the claim by the doll is usually that she has "performed services" over an extended period of time and been exclusively available to the older benefactor, causing her to become dependent on being materially cared for "at the level to which she's become accustomed" and to be unable to establish any other emotional or sexual relationships. She therefore feels entitled to be compensated for the dedication and exclusivity that is required of her by the older daddy figure.

This is perhaps the most sordid and provocative role in the inheritance drama, as so many people have an interest in the conniving and sleaziness that so often accompanies the daddy-doll relationship. What makes this kind of relationship work is mutual need. The daddy can't get the ongoing companionship he wishes simply through hiring women to go out with him. Or he is dissatisfied with his wife. And the doll cannot find anyone who will be nearly as generous with her.

Sometimes, what begins as a detached relationship of mutual benefit and/or exploitation turns into one of mutual and genuine caring and appreciation. But neither a daddy nor a doll is likely to convince anyone else around them that anything beyond money for sex, affection, and companionship is being exchanged.

One interesting aspect of this relationship from the point of view of a doll is a complication that may result over years of involvement with a sugar daddy. In my clinical practice, I have worked with women who became entangled in this kind of relationship for over a decade because they believed their daddy would keep his promise and leave his wife. What begins as an arrangement becomes a hope that the generous father figure will finally deliver not only the financial goods but the emotional goods as well.

These women came into my office asking for help to extract themselves from the relationship. This always happens when an event finally awakens them to the realization that their sugar daddy will never be leaving his marriage. They are forced to see how they have wasted many years of their adult life with the fantasy that their benefactor cared for them more than he really did. They are heartbroken when they must come to grips with the truth and see that what the sugar daddy viewed as a business arrangement became for them, the doll, a dreamy romantic escape from their own bleak future.

While some have skills that allow them to survive on their own without the money and gifts they have become accustomed to receiving, others have little going for themselves and are forced into a struggle to survive without the material lifeline that their lover provided.

After feeling controlled and used for many years, the most angry and resentful of them can't wait for the guy to die, with the continued fantasy that they will be provided for. When they're not, this becomes the final cruel blow to having given up their "best years" for a sugar daddy who ends up not delivering the final inheritance goods.

The Dedicated Caregiver: "I've been here taking care of you for so long. Could you remember who was there to do the dirty work, please?"

This is a specialized role and resembles the best friend and confidant role. However, the dedicated housekeeper/caregiver, especially one who has a long-term relationship with the trustor, may exercise even more influence on the thinking of the trustor because of the intimacy of the relationship. For those who live in the house of the trustor and also double as caregiver, the dependency formed may be even stronger than that with a good friend. Those trustors who are limited in their mobility, for example, and spend a large amount of time at home may believe that they cannot replace a housekeeper on whom they have come to trust and depend.

This kind of housekeeper may be a combination of butler/cook/medical assistant who has nursing training but who also cleans the house, cooks, drives, and helps organize bills, or any other combination of roles the trustor comes to believe are vital to the maintenance of the household and the trustor's personal freedom to stay out of a more restricted living situation.

This role lends itself to a certain degree of pressure being applied by the housekeeper, especially as the trustor becomes weaker and more dependent on her services. Short of making a play for inclusion in inheritance, it's not uncommon for the one playing this role to want more money over time as she notices the trustor becoming more dependent upon her.

Another unsavory but realistic aspect of this relationship is what may be a soft "bribe." Trustors may give generously to dissuade the housekeeper-helper from entertaining the notion of stealing money or possessions from them, especially when trustors are not able to carefully watch their home due to their condition.

My mother, for example, had someone living with her during the week for the last few months of her life, basically to help her with household chores, driving, cooking, and in case of medical emergency. She felt a certain need to be overly generous to the helper so that she would not have to be so concerned about having anything stolen from her. One way she did this was by including the person living with her in most meals and even paying for certain periods of time the person wasn't even there. The point here is that someone needing this kind of care feels very vulnerable. Even if there are family members around watching out for

her, there are plenty of opportunities for manipulative caretakers to take
advantage of the situation.

**The Deserving Charity: "Just think of how many wonderful,
deserving people your thoughtful contribution could help
once you are gone. God will reward you in heaven for your
generosity."**
This role comes up as an interesting news event occasionally, when a
church or institution is left a large gift from the estate of a wealthy benefactor. While it is uncommon for an institution to make a claim on an
estate after the death of a member, it is not so uncommon for various
groups to make their needs known and to exert whatever influence they
can on being included in a will.

Religious institutions, universities, political causes, and various
nonprofit charities come to depend on at least a portion of their revenue
coming from gifts from those who are kind enough to leave them part of
their estate when they die. This is especially likely to happen when the
trustor is quite wealthy and has more than enough to take care of family
members or has no family at all.

The problem is that these institutions are just as able to manipulate
wealthy trustors as individuals are. Some are not beyond making their
case as to how a healthy contribution will enhance the chances of the
trustor receiving prime consideration to get into the promised land. This
role is also worth mentioning because the fact is, well-to-do trustors
commonly *do* leave at least a portion of their estate to one kind of charity or personal interest group or another, depending on their affiliations
and sentiments during their lives.

This is another one of those situations where having family members be aware of their parent's plans can make a difference in the kinds
of inheritance problems that may arise after death. Upon discussion
with the parent regarding his intentions, for example, anything that
sounds out of line in the way of a gift to a charity may be questioned to
help understand the parent's thinking and to debate any plans that seem

like they may be unduly influenced by affiliations with religious groups or nonprofit charities.

Much of the manipulation regarding inheritance with charities, it should be said, is more likely to occur while the trustor is alive and involved with the group. It is in this involvement that sympathies may be played on and decisions made that later may be viewed as shortsighted, unduly influenced, and not in the best interest of the remaining family members of the trustor.

Now that we've identified the various roles played by both givers and beneficiaries, let's begin to look more closely at some of the psychological and emotional issues that are related to these roles and the various family relationships that shape the inheritance drama.

CHAPTER 4
HERE COMES YOUR
FINAL REPORT CARD

What a parent decides to leave to family members, and especially his or her children, tends to be interpreted as a final statement, or "report card," as to how the parent felt about them. No matter what the parent might say toward the end of his life to children about how he felt—or what might have been expressed earlier in life—it is what is written in the will that has the most weight emotionally—*and what the adult child never forgets*. For adult children, then, this final report card is interpreted—rightly or wrongly—as a summing up of the truest sentiment of the parent.

Beginning in early childhood and continuing through adolescence and into adulthood, siblings are waging a competitive battle with each other for a share of the limited love and attention available from their parents. In addition, they are competing for an edge to gain the approval that helps shape their early identity, self-esteem, and self-acceptance. Each child constructs a mental model of the sibling hierarchy. Whether it be by comparing physical features, intelligence, friends, skills, or accomplishments, siblings are very aware of where they stand in relation to one another. And each learns unique ways of gaining attention and favor.

It is also in the early years that they notice subtle and not so subtle differences in the treatment they receive, including who is favored or disfavored. They pay close attention to what parents tell them about where they stand and learn nonverbal behavior cues. They become experts at interpreting inconsistencies between word and deed by tuning in to tone, gesture, and innuendo. The desire to be loved and approved of by parents is the single strongest *emotional* need of the child, rivaled only by survival-level needs such as food, shelter, and physical safety.

This is how it is in all families with two or more children. Only the intensity of the competition varies among families, as well as how directly or indirectly these dynamics are played out. In single-child families, the needs of the child are the same but the competition may be focused on the parents' desire to gain the stronger bond with the child. In other words, the dynamic is focused on the triangle created between parents and child.

The closer the sibs are in age, often the stronger are the competitive feelings. Since in most families there are no more than a few years between the youngest and the eldest, the stage is set for intense competition for parental approval.

> **!** One of the main psychological themes I will reiterate periodically is *how the inheritance drama unconsciously reactivates these early competitive feelings.*

Up until the time of a family crisis, these competitive feelings are, to some degree, tempered over the course of adulthood as children mature, move out of the family home, and create their own separate lives.

Because the maturing adult learns to gain recognition and approval from his spouse, children, in-laws, friends, and work associates, he becomes less dependent on the direct approval from his parents. He also learns to be satisfied with more subtle forms of approval. He has increased the number of sources to which he may turn who will satisfy feelings of being accepted, loved, appreciated, and held in esteem.

> **!** When parents are sick and dying, early sibling rivalries may be revived, as well as the deep original childhood need for the love and approval of the parent. Because the possibility of losing the parent is more real, the adult wants to fortify feelings of being loved that have already been established, as well as make up for what he's never

adequately received. This love and approval is demonstrated in the end by how the parent chooses to deal with the child toward the end of his life and how the child is treated in his will.

When a parent is dying, adult children become concerned that they be viewed in a positive manner—no matter what the differences or problems may have been leading up to that point. In other words, the child hopes that "all's well that ends well" and wants the parent to feel the same way—whether or not it's realistic to believe that long-term resentments may be wiped away so easily. If the parent is strong enough to deal with past resentments, sometimes a mending of the relationship is possible, allowing for a sense of resolution.

Oftentimes, the predicament is such that the child doesn't want to deal with emotional material when the parent is weak or unwilling to face relationship problems. This awareness of feeling unfinished and yet not knowing how to go about bringing up the past creates tension for both parent and child.

For children, this is not a matter of scheming to receive their fair share of an inheritance but a deep desire not to have the parent die disapproving of him. This is one reason why, after the death of a parent, family members tend to initially focus on their most recent interactions with the parent, rather than the lifetime of previous experiences and memories.

We remember the final contacts with the parent most vividly and often give them an inordinate amount of attention when we think about them. For some, especially during the initial weeks after the loss of the parent, these final contacts may become obsessional. This is most likely to occur when there have been disagreements, harsh words, or only partial closure achieved before the parent's death.

We carry the notion that asking for forgiveness from a person at the end of his life can somehow alter how the dying person evaluates our previous actions. The child hopes that in his last contacts with a parent that he will be forgiven for his sins—and therefore need not feel guilty when his parent dies—for how he has disappointed the parent or failed to live up to his expectations. He wants, in other words, to "make peace" with the parent.

The adult child is also sensitive to any perceptions of inequality in the inheritance of possessions or money that would signal the parent is giving him a lesser final grade. This final grade will not only be interpreted based on what is left the child in the will, but also what gifts the parent may give in the final years, months, and days before death.

If a dying mother, for example, gives one daughter a lot of jewelry while giving nothing to her other daughter, the second daughter is very likely to interpret this as a sign of being loved less, no matter what the mother may have had in mind in her giving and no matter what she may have received along the way that would make the final actions fair and reasonable. In other words, it's the proximity to the end of life that matters here. This is one example of how emotion is more powerful than rational thought in how events are interpreted, especially when inheritance is mixed with the emotion that goes with the death of a parent.

Despite their good intentions, parents may create a problem in gifting privately or "behind the back" to one sib and not another. The sibling keeping score will likely do his best to find out who is ahead. Even though gifting privately to children while alive is a great way for parents to enjoy their gesture, there is no surefire way to keep it secret from the child who is intent on finding out. This is not a matter of need or desire on the part of the child who watches a sib receive something he doesn't. It's a matter of what the child believes is fair and equal. Remarkably, or perhaps not given the nature of human relationships, parents and children find themselves reexperiencing emotions and responses from the earliest days of their relationship.

INFLUENCING THE FINAL GRADE

Because children consciously and unconsciously want to influence the final grade their parent gives them, they may do things in the last months and years of the parent's life to improve their grade. For example, a son who has not spent what he or the parent believes is enough time with his father over the years may decide to visit his father more often, call him regularly, and listen more closely to his father's needs. He doesn't want to feel guilty for not giving his father the attention his father believes he should.

One common way children compensate for perceived past deficiencies is by devoting a concentrated period of time to caring for the parent. The child may have the parent move in with him to be able to take care of the parent in a hands-on way, or move into the parent's house for the same reason. If the parent is still in fairly healthy condition and able to travel, a vacation may be scheduled so that both parent and child will have extended time together in a positive and memorable manner.

I want to be clear about this: it's not that the child necessarily plots to "suck up" to the parent to rid himself of guilt or to improve his final grade. Sometimes, of course, it *is* intentional. But the child may consciously change his thinking to be more involved because he believes the parent needs the attention and care or because the parent asks for it or a doctor recommends it. On the other hand, some children may deem it unacceptable to consciously harbor thoughts about "sucking up" to the parent, so their behavior must be interpreted as being unconsciously motivated, no matter what their stated intention may be.

> **!** From my perspective as a psychologist, one of the things that makes the inheritance taboo so interesting is how the family dynamics may be played out at an unconscious level—*totally outside the awareness* of the family members. This is especially true because the dynamics between family members have been in process for a lifetime.

Certain ways of perceiving how other family members are operating tend to become rigid as the years pass. We think we "know" the personalities of our brothers and sisters and tend to harbor a rigid view of how they are. In the same way, we like to believe we're conscious of our own motivations when we may not be. And, as I mentioned earlier, the

unresolved rivalries that have been partially buried over the years become like old scabs that have been opened when death and dying take
over as the main event in the family drama.

FEELINGS ABOUT YOUR FAMILY

Below are a number of questions that will help you think about where
you see yourself in your family and your feelings about family members.
Answering them will help you examine past resentments with both parents and sibs. There are no right or wrong answers, nor will there be an
interpretation offered based on your responses.

Don't be in too much of a hurry to move through them and consider
writing down your answers. The intention of each cluster of questions is
not just to help clarify your thinking but to help take you deeper into ex-
amining the relationships that are relevant to your inheritance drama.

1. Do you see yourself as having close relationships with your sibs? Are
    you close enough to be able to discuss money issues with them? How
    open are you with them about the details of money issues in your
    life? How open and forthcoming are they with you about the details
    of their finances? Do you have a general idea of how much money
    they have saved? How much they earn? (Some families are open
    about this kind of information and others are not. These questions
    are all relevant to how easy or difficult it may be to discuss inheri-
    tance issues as they arise.)

2. Are you aware of favoring one sib over another? If you don't have
    close relationships, can you at least discuss family concerns such as
    health care and finances when necessary? Is it acceptable to admit
    that your feelings may not be exactly the same for all your sibs? If you
    believe you have no preferences, at least think about which sib you
    feel most similar to and in what ways. Which ones are you most dif-
    ferent from—and in which ways?

3. What is your model for where you fit in your family? Without regard
    to age, what is your standing in your family? Do your sibs contact you

regularly? Do you reach out to contact them? How often do you have passing thoughts of concern or interest for your sibs?

4. Can you identify the long-term relationship issues that exist between you and each sib? Try to state them as specifically as possible. For example, "I have always resented my sister for ignoring my accomplishments and trying to put me down by boasting about her own successes." Or: "My brothers continue to feel very competitive with me about the accumulation of material goods. They always want to know the price of everything I buy." Another example: "No matter how much I show interest in my sister's life, she almost never shows interest in what I'm doing. Even when she finally does ask, her attention span is very limited when listening to me."

   Identifying your long-term unresolved issues with sibs and parents is useful because it is *exactly* these issues that are most likely to surface during the transfer of an estate from parents to children. These same issues will continue to be played out in various forms once the parent dies and you must deal with grieving and shaping your future relationships.

5. How openly can you discuss your deeper feelings with your sibs? What happens when you discuss issues that bring up strong emotions? How much do you argue with them? How do you typically resolve differences of opinion with your sibs? Have there ever been long periods of no contact with sibs either because of strained relations or simple lack of interest?

6. Do you imagine any of your sibs would ever turn against you and create inheritance problems if they felt cheated of their rightful share? What might be the conditions for this to happen? If you don't think this could happen, what is your model of the relationship that would prevent it? How emotionally stable do you see your sibs as being?

7. How close are you to your parent or parents? Have you ever had long periods (many months or years) when you had no contact with them? If so, what were the issues that brought on the conflict that divided

you? Do you feel the issues are resolved or are they still just beneath the surface? Could they surface under the pressure of a discussion of inheritance?

8. Have your parents ever discussed their inheritance plans openly with you? If not, is there any reason these plans cannot be discussed? Have your parents ever refused to discuss their plans with you when you brought it up?

9. Have you opened discussions with your parent only to find that the discussion ended before important information was conveyed? Is so, what is it that you think your parent can't say about his or her inheritance wishes? How might you approach your parent in a way that would take the conversation further? Do you think writing down key questions you want answered would make a difference? How about reading a book (like this one) as a way to ease into discussions—do you think the person you want to talk to would read a book on such a topic?

10. What efforts have you made to learn about the legal and financial aspects of inheritance? Have you ever asked to see your parents' wills and/or trust documents? Do you think your parents would share this information with you? If yes, are you willing to ask them directly to see the papers and to discuss the contents of them, so that you may facilitate their wishes? If no, why do you think your parents won't share this important information with you?

11. Is there any difference in your mind between having medical insurance or homeowners' insurance and protecting yourself with a will? If so, how do you see them as being different? What fears would you have to overcome if you were to assertively confront your parents about their inheritance plans? Would it be worth the possibility of angering your parents to have this kind of information?

WHAT IF YOU FAIL IN YOUR FINAL GRADE?

I've said that the love and approval of parents is as powerful for the young child as any single psychological and emotional need. And yet, as mature adults, it is possible to transcend this need, at least to the point of accepting that your parents may favor one of your sibs over you. It is also possible to accept that you may fail on your final grade if your parent chooses not to include you in his will and estate inheritance.

> **!** While final rejection through exclusion is not what any child would ever wish for, standing on your own emotional feet means feeling good enough about yourself to deal with this kind of parental choice. Your total self-worth does not have to depend on whether your parent chooses to include you in his will. Most adult children who suffer through this final failing grade have been through rejection many times before. It is very unusual to have a good, strong loving relationship for a lifetime with your parent only to find that you are suddenly excluded from inheritance. Because this final parental rejection is usually the last in a long line, the child is most often not so surprised when it occurs. Nor is he totally unequipped emotionally to handle it.

Some parents simply can't save enough over the course of their lives to have much left to transfer to children. Others may have a special charity or cause to which they wish to give their money. Still others are psychologically unable to forgive and forget whatever resentments may have been created. They may take these resentments out on their children in the hurtful form of total exclusion from inheritance.

My point here is that there are a number of variables that the adult child can influence but not control that will have to do with her final report card grade. And she needs to be strong enough to deal with the possibility that exclusion from inheritance altogether, or at least not receiving a "fair" or equal share, is a real possibility.

> **!** Failing the final report card need not be equated to failing as a person or being a failure in one's life. To give any single person in our lives so much power and control to define us is a sign of a lack of ego strength and perspective. While we certainly can't help our dependence on our parents as children, we are not at all in the same helpless position as adults.

Although it is desirable for parents to give us their unconditional love and approval, it is not required. And this calls into question the whole idea of whether our parents really owe us anything at all in the way of inheritance. In other words, how have we come to believe it is our birthright that our parents transfer to us whatever they have taken a lifetime to earn and preserve?

We will explore this idea of inheritance as a birthright in Chapter 5. But before we do, we need to look at the power that parents wield through threats of disinheritance. We also need to examine how this power sometimes shapes entire lives when parents control scared and conforming children through these threats and actions.

To want things to be "fair" is to want all siblings to be treated equally by the parent. And yet it is easy to equate fairness with equality when it is no such thing! This confusion by siblings accounts for a share of the arguments that ensue upon the death of the parent. They forget that *equality does not necessarily mean fairness*. To give a simple and clear example, the child with a physical disability may clearly require more money being left for his care than other children with no disability. The parent acknowledges this need and leaves the child a larger share of the pie. This is not equal, but it's fair. While this example is easier for families to accept, it is not so easy to accept that a parent chooses to leave a child more than an equal share simply because he doesn't want it to be spent on drugs, or something else equally unacceptable.

Predictably, then, we can say that the less obvious the difference between the siblings, the greater will be the tendency for conflict to erupt when a parent doesn't leave an equal share to all involved.

CHAPTER 5
DISINHERITANCE AS A WEAPON

One of the more powerful ways that the inheritance drama affects families long before anyone dies is in the use of threats of disinheritance. Family members of the elder generations (grandparents, parents, uncles) may use various types of threats to shape the thinking and behavior of younger family members.

The early use of disinheritance threats is more prevalent in families where significant wealth has already been accumulated while children are still young and able to see conspicuous signs of it in their day-to-day lifestyle. When young children in families of wealth are taught that they need to think and behave in a certain fashion to keep their parents happy, more than just love and approval are on the line.

Although the dramas played out in wealthy families may receive far more attention from the popular media, the wealthy aren't the only ones who use the threat of disinheritance. Since wealth is obviously relative to one's social class and economic standing, the promise of an easier life through inheritance for someone who is middle class or lower middle class may have the same controlling impact as it does with the children of the wealthy.

Some would argue that it may have more impact, since those who are not well-off are more likely to hunger for an improvement in their financial standing compared to those who have known luxury since birth. The difference, of course, is that in the families of the wealthy, children grow up in and come to expect a lavish lifestyle and are therefore more immediately impacted by threats than those where future inheritance is neither so obvious nor so certain.

Whether in families of the rich or the middle class, the dynamic of control through threats of disinheritance works in a similar fashion. Either directly or through insinuation, it's made clear that conformance to the parents' wishes also means the transfer of the wealth when the parents die. Sometimes, children's knowledge that future inheritance is in the cards is the single most important long-term consideration in deciding to conform to their parents' ongoing demands. The alternative is daring to disobey and forge their own independent path, but risking the loss of any future inheritance.

The control parents exercise is not only based on the threat of disinheritance, but also on the ongoing threat of being denied the material things that the offspring wants. Young children, of course, couldn't care less about something like inheritance, which seems like an eternity away and not something they want to think about. They are far more interested and concerned with what will be given or withheld from them today, tomorrow, and next week. Because of this, the early threats in the child's life are more centered around whether the child gets what he wants in the way of clothes, toys, and the immediate satisfaction of all other material needs that are in the control of their parents.

EXAMPLE OF DISINHERITANCE THREAT

Andrea first came into my consulting office a few years ago. She wanted my help in dealing with a father by whom she felt threatened. It turns out she had good reason to feel this way. This is the story she told me.

When she was a child of about 6, her wealthy and drug-abusing father had sexually molested her on repeated occasions until she was 13. He was the head of a large corporation and had made millions of dollars over the years as the company prospered, and he exercised stock options along the way.

After pushing himself hard in his job as head of the company, his release away from work was to get high on cocaine and alcohol. He would then enter her room at the far end of their large house, where no one could hear him. Sometimes he would force Andrea to inhale a puff of marijuana to relax her and then begin fondling her body. This led to oral sex with her, demands that she fondle him, or intercourse, which was extremely painful to her. He would threaten to punish her if she cried out or dared mention his visits with her to anyone.

Andrea cried many times as she told me various parts of this story, each time feeling the pain of her father kissing her lips and pinning her down with the weight of his body. The fear, confusion, and emotional pain she experienced on so many occasions was never far from her waking awareness, even many years later. She was afraid to tell her mother or anyone else what was happening to her. Her father would bribe her by buying her expensive toys and clothes, and by giving her special attention compared to her brother. Often he would tell her that when she got older, he would give her a large amount of money.

At first, Andrea had no idea what he was talking about when he would say this. But when she got a little older, she figured out that the family was very wealthy, that her father was important in his company, and that the family's lifestyle was well beyond that of even her most well-to-do friends. She told no one about the sexual abuse. Because she didn't think her mother would believe her, she would not risk telling her the story.

Throughout her teenage years and into college, her father continued to promise her a large share of the family estate when he died, hoping to use this bribe as "hush" money. And it worked, as Andrea began to imagine her payoff for keeping quiet all these years about the sins of her father would be millions of dollars. When she would ask her father how she would get this inheritance rather than it going to her mother, he would tell her that there were specific provisions in his will that set aside a large amount just for her.

She never saw the will and didn't really believe him. But over the next twenty years, as she entered her late 40s, she looked forward to this money and not just because it would make her rich. It meant her father would be dead. And she wished for this so she would never have to look at him or be afraid of him again.

Andrea had gone on to have her own career as a successful attorney and, in her late 30s, found a man she loved and married him. It had been very difficult for her to trust men in her life, especially when it came time to be sexually intimate with them. Either she made them objects and just had casual sex with them; or, if she liked them, she held back from sexual intimacy. Predictably, after her father's abuse, the tough part was caring for a man and establishing a loving sexual relationship in which she could trust her partner.

Andrea had no psychological treatment of any kind before coming to see me. And she was in her mid-40s before finally having the courage to enter treatment. I found it interesting that she chose a male therapist, as many women who have had this kind of abuse find it easier to enter treatment with a female. When I asked her about this, she said it would be too easy to feel competitive with a woman.

Through her psychotherapy, Andrea began to see how terrified she had been of her father, even years after he had stopped sexually molesting her. She realized how much of her thinking about her family had been colored by the abuse she suffered from her father and how controlled she felt by his threats and promises. And yet, she would never stand up to him and tell him that she didn't care about his promises of future inheritance, nor would she say she didn't want his gifts. She liked what she received from him, and had come to depend on the money he sent her.

Andrea realized in her therapy that she had been so deeply traumatized through the early sexual abuse that she still did not feel able to stand up and confront her father. She wouldn't even allow herself to get angry and raise her voice to him. She had, in her own mind, made a "deal with the devil" in taking his money and gifts for so many years during and after the abuse. She would be silent in exchange for the material comforts the money provided her. And she would hope that he would someday keep his word and give her special consideration in his will when he died.

I wish I could tell you there was a happy ending to this story, but there wasn't. Andrea was forced to live in fear of her father for many years. The best she could manage was to move a few hundred miles away from him when she graduated from law school and had been offered a position in a well-regarded firm. He continued to send her money all through her 20s and 30s—money that somehow was never discussed with her mother or brother and that to this day she continues to accept from him.

The threat of disinheritance turned into the threat of stopping the payoff for silence about the past. It took her some time in therapy to deal with her guilt over taking this payoff without ever telling anyone or breaking free from her financial dependence on her father. Even when she was making enough through her own work, she still took the money her father sent her. It was the bond that connected them. She still waits patiently for her now-sickly father to die so she can claim the inheritance money that he promised her so long ago.

THE WEALTHY TRUST FUND CHILD

The threat of disinheritance from the previous example was based on bribing a child not to reveal a terrible family secret of incest. Here is a different example, showing how children of the very wealthy may have many of their life choices shaped by early knowledge of wealth and the promise of inheritance.

I worked with Tommy for many years and got to know him as well as any patient who had ever come to me. Tommy was a trust fund child born into one of the country's wealthiest blue-blooded families. He grew up on his family's private island, often isolated from other kids. He was required to dress up for formal dinner each evening, and nannies attended to him instead of his mother. When he recalled early affection shown to him, it was from simple acts of kindness from these nannies—not from his mother, who was usually too busy with her own active life of charities and entertaining to bother with much hands-on mothering.

Tommy did everything possible to fail out of one fancy prep school after another. Each time his parents used their influence to get him into new one, he always found a way to defeat their best efforts. Feeling desperate to compete with his siblings for his parents' limited time and affection, his calculated aim was to get their attention any way possible. His thinking: If he couldn't get it by being good, he'd get it by being bad. And it worked.

Because of his family's vast fortune, he figured out at an early age that it didn't matter how he did in school because someday he was going to inherit millions of dollars. He was only vaguely threatened by his parents that his inheritance would be withheld if he didn't perform up to their expectations. Instead, they withheld their love and refused to support his half-baked schemes and projects.

The knowledge that there would be a large inheritance gave Tommy a financial safety net beneath all of his choices. If he failed, so what? The family inheritance was always going to be there to catch his fall. After dropping out of college because of poor grades, he served in the Navy, then had a very short marriage of which his parents disapproved.

Later he had a girlfriend and from this relationship came his only biological child, a child with whom he had little contact for many years after his romantic relationship with her mother soured. His work history was spotty and was typified by trying a number of things that never worked out the way he had hoped.

Tommy received a few million dollars when his mother died. He was in his 30s at the time. He then more seriously threw himself into his career as a heavy-drinking playboy, priding himself on attracting many sexual partners. Finally, Tommy had found something he was good at. He could be charming when he wanted to be, had a good sense of humor, and had a fantasy of doing stand-up comedy. In fact, it was his habit of trying to disarm me with humor that always let me know we had touched a sensitive issue that he wished to avoid.

Despite the pleasure and bravado that accompanied his preoccupation with bedding women, Tommy struggled to engage in meaningful interests or work that might help him find himself. His mother had often referred to him as a "lounge lizard," an old-fashioned term that hurt him deeply. But he knew it was true. She compared him mercilessly to his more successful siblings, even though all of them were having personal problems as a result of growing up in this family. His rejecting and distant father was even worse, totally unable to praise him in any way and disapproving of any efforts he later made in starting and managing a number of businesses.

Tommy expressed disdain for the nouveau riche, whom he viewed as practicing conspicuous consumption to impress others who had made it. He went to the opposite end of the spectrum, concealing anything about his own heritage or finances that might reveal his identity. He believed if others knew of his wealth, they would try to take advantage of him.

He dressed casually, sometimes sloppily, and liked shopping at cheap discount clothing stores. He prided himself on "getting a deal" for furniture and other things, much of which wasn't worth buying. He bought a fancy home right on the beach but never cared to unpack all his belongings or properly furnish his home. And he could be stingy and small-minded in his thinking and spending habits. For example, before the era of all-you-can-use free cell phone minutes, he and his sibs made a practice of sending each other itemized bills for long-distance calls made when they stayed with one another as guests.

It took me months to convince him that he could easily afford to fly business class on long trips. I knew I'd finally gotten through to him when, years into our work together, he began flying on the expensive chartered flights that some Hollywood stars favor. Once he sat across from Candice Bergen, he was sold on this type of flying.

But Tommy could also be quite generous. I had known him to assist friends of lesser fortune in life when they needed help. He carefully sheltered his family name from most of his friends; some knew him for years and didn't know to whom he was related.

In the same vein, Tommy could date a woman for months and never say a word about his financial condition. Understandably, he never wanted to be liked just for his money. He didn't want to let the cat out of the bag, fearing that if people knew his family pedigree, they would never accept him for himself but only for his wealth. And he feared being seen as a failure.

This became one of the ongoing themes of our work together. In over ten years of psychotherapy, he gradually freed himself from this sense of failure. He was finally able to choose to give up drugs and alcohol, stop womanizing, and pursue his interest in the theater. Now, many years later, he sends me notices of the plays he is cast in. He has stayed sober and is much more content with himself and his life, even though he never managed to find the love of his life and marry. I interpreted his never marrying again as a continued fear of what price he would have to pay—both emotionally and financially—if it didn't work out.

CONFRONTING THE DISINHERITANCE ISSUE

As the above two stories have shown, the threat of disinheritance means that a child is forced to decide how much he is willing to have his thinking and actions controlled by a future possibility. Here are some questions that those facing this threat must answer:

1. How important to my financial survival or everyday convenience is the money or possessions that are being threatened?
2. Can I imagine living without the inheritance and not feeling resentful?
3. How important is it to make choices that help me become my own person if they clash with the choices I'd have to make not to risk losing an inheritance?
4. Could I sacrifice forging my own path, without shame and loss of self-respect, if I know it means compromising my values and integrity?
5. Can I imagine standing up to the threatening parent or relative and taking my chances of disinheritance? Or does this seem like too much of a risk?
6. How much of my daily life revolves around fears of loss of my parents' love and approval? To what degree do I interpret their threat as a statement of a lack of love and approval?
7. How dependent on my parents' financial help have I become over the years? Can I imagine feeling secure if I was left nothing?

8. How much have I borrowed from my parents and never paid back or not paid back in full so that they may make things more "even" by not leaving me as much as my siblings? Would I interpret this as being disinherited or unfair?

9. Would I feel resentment toward my siblings if they received something in the way of possessions or money and I didn't? Can I separate my siblings from my parent so that I would not blame my siblings for a decision that was not theirs?

10. Would I expect them to share something they receive if nothing was left to me? Would I expect them to share and make it "fair" if anyone is left more than me, or could I accept my parent's choice?

THE CONCEPT OF FAIRNESS

One of the reasons the threat (or reality) of disinheritance is such a bitter pill to swallow is that it rests on the notion of fairness. Children have grown up not only with the idea that they should be equally loved by their parents but also that all that parents have in the way of money and possessions should be *equally and fairly* shared with all siblings, regardless of their actual need. Both while they are alive and when they die, the idea of fairness is fundamental to children's thinking.

What is fair is always a matter of perception. Because of this, it is always open to disagreement and argument. To complicate the issue, fairness is not the same as equality. For example, one child may be much more in need of help than another. Giving more to this child may be "fair" in the thinking of parents but not equal in the amounts of money given in the way of loans to each child. We will return to the issue of fairness in the next chapter; I introduce it here simply to point out how important it is in shaping the thinking and reactions of children to their parents' decision regarding money and possessions. In the parent's mind there is always a reason for deciding to disinherit a child—whether or not the child understands or agrees with it.

WHAT IF YOU'RE DISINHERITED?

The best way to deal with the threat of disinheritance is to *expect nothing* from your parents' estate when they die. If you have taken care of yourself well enough over the years with your own earnings and savings, you will only need to deal with the emotional aspects of being disinherited—not the desperation that comes with the realization that the windfall you were expecting is not going to materialize.

Here is an example of a trust fund child who decides to sever the relationship with his mother rather than remain under her control through the threat of disinheritance, or an inheritance that must be "earned."

My husband's family is wealthy, that is, his mother. She lives in Palm Springs with her husband and has a second home in Jacksonville. I've never met her and probably never will. You see, my husband and she are estranged due to the money.

Originally his grandmother had left him a tidy sum but rather than putting it in trust, she left her daughter, his mother, in control. His mother chose to pretend the inheritance did not exist and refused to honor it. That caused a problem.

His brother, who is willing to kowtow to the mother's every whim, will receive whatever inheritance she may dole out, although the woman apparently is spiteful and may choose to instead cut him off, too. Some people, even in death, are not to be trusted.

When I first met my husband he told me his mother was dead. That's a pretty strong statement to make when it is untrue. He had been living off a trust fund and his mother was pulling the strings, turning the spigot on and off at will if he displeased her.

The point of this message is that many who have families with money choose to "give it up" in favor of having their own lives. Apparently some with substantial funds to leave their children believe it gives them license to run the lives of those children while they're alive and even after death by deciding who they may or may not marry, etc. Some choose to say no.

My husband is better off psychically for letting go of the idea of "money to come" by waiting for someone he despises to die. Mean people don't die young. What goes around comes around gone wrong.

Another way to deal with threats by parents is to decide what we are willing to do to comply with their expectations and demands and what we are unwilling or unable to do. This is the process of compromise— both with our own idealistic values and with the needs of family members. And it is a process we play out over the life of the family relationship. It's what the above questions are aimed at helping to determine. Also useful is an examination of our beliefs about what we are owed, which we will look at in the next chapter.

The emotional part of the threat of disinheritance is for some the most difficult to deal with. Although we may have come to expect something in the way of inheritance, it is the feeling of being emotionally abandoned by the parent's decision not to leave money or possessions that we may find most difficult to accept.

If you are actually disinherited in your parent's will, you can always hire a lawyer to contest it. But you should know that most parents who decide to take this drastic step to specifically disinherit a child have usually done it with careful consideration and with the help of an attorney. The odds are heavily against you if you decide to contest the will, unless you have some legal basis beyond just feeling it's "unfair."

We need to keep in mind that in the greater percentage of families, the amounts of money and personal and real property being transferred are not going to drastically change the lifestyle of the children once they receive their inheritance. For most of us, at best, we will add a cushion to our own savings and perhaps allow for some short-term indulgence that otherwise would not have been possible.

Supporting this assertion is a 1993 study by two Cornell University economists, in which it was estimated that the average estate passed to heirs would be worth $90,000. Because this $90,000 is an average, it means many will be receiving significantly less. Remember, this is the *total* estate—which means for example that it will be divided by three if there are three beneficiaries.

Only in the wealthiest families will the amounts be large enough to make a substantial difference. Baby boomers transferring their wealth to their own children over the next thirty years will be more significant—not so much what they receive from their parents. According to one study done in 1999 by the Social Welfare Research Institute at Boston College, more than six million estates of $1 million and above will be inherited by the children of boomers.

This means that what is really being transferred to the greater percentage of boomers from their parents is more of a financial supplement to what the child already has been able to save, as well as the meaningful personal possessions that have symbolic value in keeping children connected to the parent.

In terms of disinheritance, then, what is being played out is the most severe form of rejection that the child could be given. It is an embarrassing slap in the face from the child's point of view. The insult of receiving nothing in the way of money or personal property is compounded by the emotional injury of the parents' rejection. *It is this emotional component that can continue to affect the child for years, even the rest of his life,* even when the need for material goods is limited or nonexistent.

One way to say this is, "I can handle that you chose not to leave me any of your money or your possessions. But I can't handle that you could reject me so deeply as your child and do something like this to me."

With all this in mind, in the next chapter I ask important questions about your expectations regarding anyone owing you any kind of inheritance.

CHAPTER 6
THINK INHERITANCE IS YOUR
BIRTHRIGHT? THINK AGAIN!

N ow we get down to the nitty-gritty of inheritance expectations. One reason for discussing threats of disinheritance in the last chapter was to point us toward questioning the underlying assumption that we are owed anything at all. In doing so, we'll look at how the concept of fairness comes into play in our expectations.

We'll especially look at our expectations in light of the sense of entitlement that is one of the defining characteristics of the baby boomer generation and how it influences our beliefs about what we deserve. I will offer insight into *why* this notion of inheritance as a birthright is so hard to overcome.

Let's begin by simply stating the reality that statistics tell us about the amount of money typically inherited. Although some estimate that $41 trillion will pass to baby boomers between 1995 and 2045 and other estimates have been as high as $136 trillion, much of this money is controlled by a very small percentage of wealthy families. The common statistic quoted estimates that 37 percent of the nation's wealth is controlled by 5 percent of the households. If you are fortunate enough to fall within that 5 percent, perhaps you have nothing to worry about—at least financially—and can instead focus on the emotional issues involving a parent's death.

Everyone else beyond this 5 percent will be hoping for an inheritance that simply may not add up to anything near what they are expecting. In addition, a study released in 2000 by the Federal Reserve Bank of Cleveland calculated from a 1998 federal Survey of Consumer Finances that 92 percent of those people receiving inheritances received virtually nothing, while a very small 1.6 percent received more than $100,000. For those who are expecting to fund their retirement through inheritance, these statistics suggest most will be disappointed.

HOW DO WE COME TO EXPECT AN INHERITANCE?

The poor odds of receiving substantial inheritance do not stop our expecting to receive something. How have we come to expect that we are entitled to receive anything from our family members when they die?

First, the obvious. It is built into our biology and genetics that a blood relationship is the strongest physical bond people may share with each other. All of this is true *before* human emotions come in to complicate the picture. The power of conflicted emotion may ultimately override close family ties with jealousies, resentments, and disagreements that may turn into full-fledged blood wars. But we start with an understanding that sharing the same blood means we have something important in common.

We then assume that those who have brought us into the world will do their very best to care for us—not only while they are alive but after they die, through what they leave us, as well. We assume this because we want to believe that our parents will love and care for us more than anyone else in the world. We consider it their *duty* to provide for us in every way possible, as part of the obligation that comes with good parenting.

Growing up and spending our early years dependent on our parents, relatives, and siblings helps us know and trust these people and strengthens our bond with them. In a reasonably healthy and intact family, this is how it unfolds, more or less. Through sharing and coping during years of various kinds of experiences—economic survival, health-related emergencies, various developmental milestones, and the sharing of secrets, celebrations, vacations, and simple day-to-day living—family members come to feel a deepening connection and sense of responsibility for the welfare of one another. The values expressed and demonstrated by elders of the family and the community, including so-cial and religious institutions, reinforce this connection.

But it is exactly *because* of the powerful emotional and psychologi-cal connections that feelings of jealousy and resentment, and the need to control by having one's own way, may predominate when family members try to deal with events like death and inheritance. In some families, the loss of a parent—especially the second parent where the children are now on their own—draws the siblings closer together, at least initially. And in others, it marks the beginning of a pulling apart, as the parental "glue" that held them together is no longer there.

> **[!]** We view inheritance as an entitlement because we're taught that love means giving. And giving means passing on, or trans-ferring from one generation to another everything of value, so that a family name and genetic bloodline may survive. This gives us a sense of immortality, of living "forever" through our children and future gen-erations. Wouldn't we want to leave to those whom we are most con-nected whatever will make their lives easier and, at the same time, enable us to imagine immortality when we die?

I've heard many older people say, as they reflected upon having lived full lives and began thinking about death, that the most important thing for them was to be remembered by their family and friends and to have something of themselves to pass down to their children. To state the obvious: One of the psychological reasons for having children is the wish to continue to have some trace of one's existence beyond one's own death. Individual lives are made more meaningful through the family unit and all the joys and sorrows that accompany raising children to adulthood. Children and extended family create the primary meaning in life for many, the unit in which their most basic needs for love, affec-tion, security, support, and guidance are met.

The family unit is also an economic survival force, where the group of relatives help each other in the struggle to make their financial way

and the efforts of the unit are more effective than the efforts of each separate individual. While this economic survival unit is not as tight as it
was in past generations when family businesses were more prevalent, it's
still part of inheritance thinking.

You know most of this already. But we need to mention it as contributing to our expectation of inheritance. Given this, no wonder so
many think first of this most important social unit when we pass on.

The stability and cohesion created by a family name, common history, and sharing of financial resources to sustain the unit become core
aspects of one's individual identity and security. Some families like to
trace their history, constructing a family tree to get a sense of that history
through many generations. They feel connected to the past through
identification with their ancestors and take pride in family crests, leg-
ends, and traditions.

This core identification with roots is further exemplified in the
search that some adopted children undertake to discover their biological
parents. They want to know "where they came from," and the importance of their biological parents may become an obsessive preoccupation, even when they've had a secure upbringing with their adopted
parents. I've heard adoptees express a lack of rootedness and a nagging
sense of only partial self-identity. They want to find their place in the
world—a place oriented by where they've come from—which is difficult to do for those who go through their lives without knowledge of one
or both of their biological parents.

My point is simple: If the formation of our self-identity and at least
a portion of our personal security rest on our family identity, we wish to
sustain this identity when we think about what we will leave to those
closest to us. And, at the same time, we wish to strengthen the family
identity in those to whom we leave it.

Besides acting as the bearers of family history and desiring to pass
this history down to our children and grandchildren, I mentioned above
that we think we'll "live on," finding a form of immortality, through
what we pass on to our family. We wish to pass down our own personal
values as to what it means to live the good and just life and some of the

knowledge and wisdom we have managed to accumulate. And, of course, we wish to transfer the fruits of our labor in the form of money, real estate, and personal possessions—at least when there has not been a major rupturing of the relationship to children along the way.

ENTITLEMENT: FROM THE CHILD'S POINT OF VIEW

Now let's approach the sense of inheritance entitlement from the point of view of the child. Especially for us baby boomers, the sense of entitlement to an inheritance is quite strong. Most don't even question that they "deserve" whatever their parents have managed to accumulate. Not only do we feel deserving, we also believe we ought to have what we want when we want it. We have come to expect that we shouldn't have to wait for what we want, so finding methods that provide for this immediate gratification of desires has led us to live on charge cards, bank loans, and gifts from parents.

For example, the recent method of choice for indulging in immediate gratification may be seen in the tidal wave of home mortgage refinancing. Millions of us in various regions throughout the country have watched the value of our homes climb for the last few years. We may have taken advantage of record-low interest rates to refinance our mortgages. But rather than allowing their equity to build by taking out a new loan for the same amount at a lower rate, some have instead chosen to take out chunks of cash, spending it on supporting their lifestyle and extending themselves even further. While "cashing out" from a refinance makes sense if we use it to pay off credit card debt or to renovate the house, it is not wise to support an indulgent lifestyle that we really can't afford. This, of course, does not stop millions of boomers from doing it anyhow. They are going to have it *now*—anyway they can manage it.

Curiously, some boomers seem not to assume that what is good for the goose is good for the gander. Although they believe they are owed inheritance by their parents, they don't necessarily believe they owe their *own* children. Their desire to indulge in having what they want when they want it may push them to spend everything they have during their own lifetimes. We will go further into this "spend-it-while-you're-alive" mentality at the end of this chapter.

> ⚠ Entitlement, a key characteristic of narcissism, can make for some real problems. Narcissists believe others ought to make them the center of the universe. They have a very "me"-centered perspective that is unable to make much room for others being the center of their own individual universe. Depending on the severity of the self-centeredness, the narcissist may refuse to comprehend that parents, siblings, friends, and the rest of the world are not simply satellites existing to satisfy his or her needs and desires.

Here's an extended example of how a sense of entitlement and narcissism develop and are later played out when it comes time for inheritance. Difficulties in dealing with her family brought Lisa, 48, to my office. She grew up as the third child of four in a close family that enjoyed many of the comforts of an upper-middle-class lifestyle. She never worried about having enough of the material things that kids want, and she had plenty of friends.

A better than average student in high school and college, Lisa still struggled with her studies, which didn't come easy for her. Nor did she have much aptitude for business or personal finance. But this did not stop her from wanting to begin her own business a few years after graduating from college.

Because she had learned how to get her parents to give her what she wanted, her two sisters and brother viewed her as charming but manipulative, someone who thought about her own desires and not much about theirs.

With a loan from her father and two other passive partners, she began a technology-related business when she graduated. Because she felt she would have a better chance somewhere with less competition, she decided to move from her original home. She had been married briefly in her 30s, and had one child from that marriage who was now a teenager. While she had always been viewed by her sibs and friends as unconventional in her thinking and dress, she was not so far to the extreme to not be able to fit in when she wanted to. She had a caring and sentimental side that was attractive and that was readily apparent as I got to know her through our work together.

Through her hard efforts, her business was successful enough to survive and, for brief periods, even thrive. Unfortunately, whenever she seemed to be getting ahead, she had a history of making bad financial decisions that defeated her best efforts. This was complicated by the fact that she was not good at reaching out to get guidance from consultants and experts when she needed it. She liked to believe that she knew more than she really did—not only about finances but about many other areas as well.

I noticed, for example, that when I tried to offer her a new way to look at something, she would either tell me she already had considered it or would dismiss it as not worthy of her consideration. It could take her months to finally hear my interpretations and allow them to sink in. And it could take months longer for her to be able to apply them by changing her behavior. Too often, by the time she was ready to act on information, it was too late; opportunity had passed her by.

More than once, an employee ended up stealing from her because she wasn't watching the accounting books closely enough. She took out loans that she had trouble repaying and made investments that cost her much of her savings when the market plunged.

Lisa had disputes with landlords that cost her attorneys' fees she couldn't afford because she refused to compromise. She was quite set in her ways, resisting anything that threatened her own beliefs. She liked to indulge in shopping, which resulted in credit card debt. Because there was no marital partner in her life, she had no one to put checks and balances on her thinking when she wanted to indulge her impulses. This led to some bad decisions, buying things she couldn't really afford. She had difficulty saving much for her own future or the future college education of her child.

Lisa's judgment was also poor when it came to dating partners and boyfriends, resulting in trouble achieving satisfying relationships.

Although the relationships started out with promise, after a few months the men she chose began to see that Lisa needed to be in control. When they were passive, it worked for a while. But sooner or later, they either rebelled, creating emotional struggles, or they just decided to throw in the towel and leave.

When I asked Lisa why she thought she had trouble with men, she would blame them for not understanding her and appreciating how creative she was. She thought of herself as a "free spirit," and any man who tried to rein her in was met with her stubborn unwillingness to compromise. She told me she'd rather be alone and just have boyfriends she could occasionally have sex with than give up her freedom by conforming or compromising to the needs of another.

The truth was, I could see Lisa liked living on the edge, even when it put her in personal, financial, or legal jeopardy. One of the reasons she could get away with living on the edge was that someone was always there, keeping her from falling too far: her father.

When she got into financial trouble, she relied on her father to bail her out by sending her money. He sent ongoing gifts of thousands of dollars to help Lisa pay for the expenses in raising her child and to support her lifestyle. These gifts did not escape the notice of her three sibs, all of whom were taking care of themselves financially and did not ask for help that they didn't pay back.

Lisa had come to expect her father to bail her out in times of trouble and never could afford to pay back the money he would send her. With her sense of entitlement, she viewed the money not as a loan but as a gift. And she had some reason to view it this way, as her father did not make it clear that paying him back was to be taken seriously. He felt sorry for her and wanted to help her raise her child, knowing that Lisa was far away and on her own, while the other sibs were all married and doing well.

Her father had been living in the house that Lisa and her sibs had grown up in and owned it free and clear, after living there for over forty years. Her mother had died some time ago. When her father died, Lisa decided that she wanted to buy the house from her siblings so she could come back to work and live there part time if she wished. She liked the idea of keeping the house in the family, and thought it would provide her the means to have an ongoing relationship with her siblings, who still resided within a few hours of the home. But she didn't want to give up the house she already owned to make it possible to afford the family house.

Because she had come to expect her father to support her in every way possible—from his money to his backing of even her poor decisions— she couldn't understand why her siblings wouldn't continue the same enabling treatment when it came time to deal with the family home. Lisa expected them to sell her the house at an unrealistically low price. Even when given three months before it went on the market, she re-fused to comply with the deadlines set for her. She wanted to buy it on her terms only, and then was outraged when the executor of the estate fi-nally put it on the open market. Even then, Lisa could have bought it but continued to refuse to comply with any loan requirements as well as the deadlines set.

Her sibs, who initially tried to be understanding of her way of cop-ing with grieving, became increasingly aggravated by her accusations that they were taking advantage of her and her inability to see they, too, had needs and that they would not continue the enabling special treat-ment of their father.

Lisa had constructed the notion over many years that it was very im-portant for her be able to come back to the house she grew up in. She equated keeping the house in the family with continuing the "legacy" of the family. But she couldn't accept that her sibs were going to get the full value of the house on the open market, rather than give it to her at a price far less than it was worth.

This is what a sense of entitlement is all about.

Lisa was difficult to deal with, stomping away from her siblings when they tried to reason with her and hanging up the phone when she was given the least resistance to having her way. She felt they were "out to get her" and trying to "rip her off" simply because they refused to hand her the most valuable asset of the inheritance without assurance she could afford it.

Because their father had put the house and the rest of his assets in a trust, they feared having to have the house foreclosed on if they allowed her to get in over her head. It was at this point that she came to see me, wanting me to help her sort out her reactions to her sibs. She fought me, too, not wanting to hear that she was being unreasonable with her sibs to expect they would care more about her desires than their own.

Her inability to comprehend that her siblings did not really care whether the house stayed in the family but wished to get the highest value possible for it, and her resentment when they refused to give her the same preferential treatment that her father had, all had to do with her grandiose sense of entitlement. Her emotional investment in the house blinded her from being able to approach it as a business deal, where she was not entitled to be handed a second home to live in on a part-time basis, *just because she wanted it.*

When I had a family counseling session, I learned that all three of her sibs had come to be very cautious of entering into any business arrangements with Lisa. They had seen the trouble she had in managing her business affairs and her divorce and did not want to put the largest asset of their father's estate in her hands when they didn't think she could handle the responsibilities of paying for it.

Her father, in bending over backward to accommodate his fear of Lisa being unable to make her own way, ended up enabling her to never assume personal responsibility for her own poor decisions. My work with Lisa entailed trying to break through her stubborn and fixed ideas about her siblings being out to hurt her and her sense of entitlement. I tried to show her that just because her sibs did not want to accommodate her didn't mean they were trying to "rip her off" or were otherwise acting against her. They simply did not want to "give away the farm" so that Lisa could have a second home when they were concerned about caring for their own homes.

The price her siblings had to pay for not accommodating her on her terms was her alienating herself from them and creating a breach that was not to be repaired for many years. She had demonstrated that when push came to shove, she allowed her emotional problems to dominate logic and clear thinking. And perhaps worse, she had made enemies of her own brother and sisters.

> **!** One point of this story is that the psychological dynamics that have been in play over the lifetime of the family will not only continue but *may become exaggerated* when the death of a parent and inheritance come into the picture.

Whatever mistrust has been brewing beneath the surface among sibs will tend to bubble up and come into play, touched off by dealing with grief and mourning. This is complicated by the fact that the motivation for much of what is being played out is outside the awareness of each of the participants.

When a child has played out a particular enabling dynamic with a parent, such as expecting special treatment from the world because the parent has treated the child this way, it is not surprising that the child transfers this expectation to his or her siblings. But there is more going on than just what a parent has done that influences children's reactions during inheritance.

THE RETURN OF THE NEED TO BE NURTURED

The child is, of course, dependent on his parents—especially his mother—to survive through childhood and into adolescence. Besides the child needing parents to satisfy his physical needs, he also relies on them for emotional needs, to provide a constant nurturing that makes for a safe and secure environment.

As the child matures, he continues to rely on his parents for these emotional and psychological needs, even as physical survival becomes less conditional on them. The emotional bond with parents in a healthy family means that he strives for love, approval, and recognition. For some, as they move into adulthood and even into their 30s and 40s, there is also a lingering need and/or desire to be assisted financially along the way. The dependence on parents takes the form of loans and gifts, to ensure the child's comfort and well-being even when that child becomes an adult. In other words, the child never loses his attachment to the parents. But the form those attachments take may change over the years.

> **!** What happens when a parent dies, and especially the second parent, is that children are (usually unconsciously) thrust back into infantile needs for protection and nourishment. Part of what makes ripping oneself away from the parent so difficult is that the child has fantasies of being cared for as long as he or she lives. The death of the parent means this will not happen. It also means that any unmet needs for love and affection will *never* be met and must now be given up. ·

> **!** *This means that we not only mourn the loss of the parent but also the unfulfilled needs the parent represents.*

The awareness of this desire to reexperience the nourishment from the parent, especially a mother, may not hit us immediately. But it affects our mourning immediately, even if unconsciously. And it may affect how clearly we are able to think when it comes time to deal with siblings and the estate inheritance.

> **!** Children may experience the need to inherit money and personal possessions quite strongly as a substitute for the physical affection and psychological and emotional nourishment that is no longer directly provided by the parent. We might put it like this: "If you can't be here to take care of me yourself, at least continue to nourish me through what you leave me."

We interpret this need as part of what we think is "owed" to us by the parent, and thus come to feel entitled to an inheritance as a continuation of the nurturing process. Some of this sense of entitlement comes from the belief that the parent wants us to continue to be given whatever we need to help survive the loss. If this longing for continued nurturance by the parent is conscious, we may factor it into our reactions to siblings and other family members in dealing with inheritance issues.

In the same way, we may consider disinheritance as the parent's statement that he will no longer play the nurturing role, which we equate to "You no longer love me or want to take care of me."

GIVING UP THE EXPECTATION OF INHERITANCE

Because we unconsciously expect to be taken care of forever, we assume we can't bear the reality of being disinherited. And yet one of the signs of the healthy, mature, and independent adult is the ability to *give up any expectation of inheritance of any kind*.

It is one thing to accept graciously what parents give us before or after they die because that is their wish. It is another to *expect* something or become *attached* to getting anything in particular. We need to remember that although the will of a parent may be his final statement, we don't have to use that legal document to define our relationship with him. We may instead remember our whole lifetime of experience with that person to define what we had.

Obviously, this isn't easy to do. But it leaves room for us to accept that the final report card need not necessarily define our final grade — that our final grade is, in the end, something we must determine *ourselves* and not necessarily something that material inheritance measures.

> **!** To truly give up any expectation means that we've put ourselves in a place in our lives where we view anything we receive in the way of money or possessions as a welcome supplement to what we have managed to provide for ourselves. I want to suggest, then, that relying on an inheritance is based on an inability to stand on our own financial and emotional feet, combined with the infantile wish to be taken care of *forever* by parents. When you don't need anything from your parents, you are less likely to get caught in a struggle with sibs or other family members if it doesn't turn out the way you want it to.

Can you imagine how much psychological suffering could be avoided if people could give up their expectation of inheritance? How many families would have stayed together if individuals didn't let their attachment to what they think they deserve result in blood wars that have ripped them apart? And how irrational and sad it is when so many of these family wars are fought over relatively small amounts of money or personal property that is mostly sentimental in value?

We all mourn the loss of the nurturing and attachment we once had to our parents. This attachment is normal and expected, and the loss of it needs to be mourned. But should we believe that we are no more able to take care of ourselves now, as adults, than we were back as children or young adults? Or at least to act as if that were true?

> **!** *The death of a parent tends to reactivate infantile longings.* The stronger the bond of nurturance and the more giving the parent (especially a mother), the more powerfully these feelings will be activated. For a father, it may be more a focus on safety and security needs and questions of whether you can stand on your own feet in the world. If you consider this, it will help you make sense of much of what you may experience emotionally and in your thoughts and fantasies in the early weeks and months following the loss of your parent.

YOUR OWN FEELINGS OF ENTITLEMENT

Use the following questions to help clarify your own thoughts and feelings about being entitled to an inheritance. It is best to read the questions and notice if any quick answers come up. Then come back to them later after you have had some time to think about them.

1. When you read the story about Lisa and her being so caught up with her own needs, what was your response?
2. How much could you relate to feeling similarly to Lisa in her thinking?
3. What has your family history taught you that leads you to believe you

are entitled to an inheritance from your parents, grandparents, or other family members?

4. What family dynamics are you aware of that might make receiving what you believe is your fair share of an inheritance problematic?

5. Are you willing to consider that your sense of entitlement may be based on psychological factors, such as the desire to be taken care of forever by your parents?

6. Are you willing to consider that no matter what you believe you're entitled to, your parents and sibs may not agree with you? Have you left room in your thinking for this disagreement, and are you prepared to compromise?

7. Have you been honest with yourself about *why* you feel entitled to an inheritance?

8. Are you willing to consider that the strongest position of emotional and psychological strength is to let go of any need for inheritance?

9. If not, what emotional price would you be willing to pay should you need to confront your siblings and other family members?

10. What insights do you have about yourself and your relationships with your sibs that you can use to help understand the drama that may be played in your family around inheritance? (Question 4 has to do with how *others* are; now I'm asking you to look at yourself.)

"WE'RE SPENDING OUR CHILDREN'S INHERITANCE"

As the statistics I cited earlier indicated, a significant percentage of children inherit little or nothing from their parents. It has been this way through all previous generations, although the amounts of money up for inheritance are increasing for the boomer generation, both from their parents and what boomers themselves will leave to their children. But the choices of *how* they give are changing, and that's what we'll now examine.

In past generations, inheritance of any consequence was a luxury reserved for the wealthy. The stories related to inheritance that captured the imagination were of interest because they made public the financial machinations in the families of the rich, famous, and powerful. Large amounts of money and property were at stake, and the battles between family members were seen as well worth fighting. Since there was so much at stake, greediness and entitlement entered the process, turning siblings and relatives against each other and making them enemies. Of course, it is much the same today, except that there is a far larger middle class that has savings as well as personal and real property to transfer to heirs.

I've argued in this chapter that it is best not to expect an inheritance from your parents or any other family members. I've suggested that it is a sign of psychological and financial maturity not to need anything of a material nature and certainly not to depend on it.

Now I want to give an example that will show what can happen when you *do* expect something, but your parents happen not to be thinking the same way—in other words, they are not interested in leaving you anything, at least in the form of inheritance. This thinking isn't mainstream and most likely never will be. But it is indicative of an alternative view of how to deal with accumulated wealth and personal property. Further, it's a good example of how inheritance thinking changes to fit changes in a family's economics. It is a philosophy that has been adopted by a segment of the generation who are the parents to boomers. And it will, no doubt, be adopted by a percentage of boomers themselves and the generations to follow.

In Chapter 2, we identified the squanderer as one of the types of trustors (or givers) when it comes to dealing with money and possessions. We said that the perpetual squanderer has a history of being unable to save money or think about the future. This person is a poor bet for his children when it comes to having much to pass down, having decided that he either needs every nickel he has just to survive, or wants to spend whatever extra he manages to accumulate on himself. This type goes against the grain of their generation if they are the parents of boomers, as the more common philosophy Depression-era children adopted has been a sense of obligation to leave something for *their* children.

We also said that there is a squandering "lite" type, where clearly

the issue is not the ability to manage money, but of personal philosophy. That philosophy may best be typified by the bumper sticker that
reads, "We're Spending Our Children's Inheritance." This is not just a
cute saying or a cruel joke. It is a true statement of intention and practice. A growing number from generations who are now in their 60s and
70s—as well as the boomer generation next in line—are questioning
the traditional wisdom of slaving for a lifetime simply to have enough
saved to live through retirement and then pass on whatever is left to
their children.

We are questioning the sense of obligation to children. And not
only are we questioning it on a philosophical basis, we are challenging
it on financial grounds. Some have argued that it is not good financial
planning or money management to save up and then transfer your estate
through a will or trust.

This philosophy of spending your wealth while you are alive was
made popular by a best-selling book in 1997 entitled *Die Broke* by
Stephen M. Pollan. Pollan argued that there are tax benefits to gifting
your money to your family while you are alive, rather than leaving the
money as inheritance when you die. He believes it is foolish to pursue
what he calls "financial immortality" by wanting to leave inheritance.

He views the desire to establish an estate as a holdover from an earlier age that leads to unnecessary sacrifices far outweighing the future
benefits. He believes that the fear of dying broke is "a twentieth-century
fear carried forward into twenty-first-century life," and derived from financial patterns from the Great Depression.

Pollan's plan for wealth management and prosperity is made up of
four provocatively labeled items. First, under what he calls "quit your
jobs," he suggests that you separate yourself mentally from your em-
ployer and think of yourself as an independent agent, who isn't loyal to
anyone but himself. Given that most corporations no longer have any
loyalty to their employees, this idea is practical and survival oriented in
an age when people are forced to "reinvent" themselves, moving from
one career to another.

Second, Pollan suggests paying cash for everything possible, rather than relying on credit cards that, when mismanaged, put you in debt. Here he simply reiterates the wise advice not to live beyond your means. Earlier, I made the same point in discussing how boomers' desire for immediate gratification has caused them to bury themselves in various forms of debt.

One topic he covers under this item is what had been the common practice of "serial homeownership": moving up from one house to a more expensive one and viewing your home as an investment, capitalizing on rapid appreciation to help you move up. He doesn't like this practice, believing people should move to their final, "downsized" home as their first home—not their last. In other words, buying one home you can afford and living in it the rest of your life. Pollan published his book in 1997. Although it may have been arguable then that real estate was not a rapidly appreciating investment, it isn't the case now.

As I write this, midway through 2003, the housing market has been so good that some housing analysts consider the remarkable price appreciation a "bubble" waiting to burst. Homes have appreciated in some parts of the country over the last year at the rate of 20 to 40 percent, and interest rates on home loans have never been lower. It makes no sense, then, to claim—as Pollan did six years ago—that houses aren't a good investment or that you shouldn't consider moving up to the most expensive house you can afford, viewing it as a long-term investment (at least five to ten years) that may be enjoyed as you make it a home.

In addition, changes in the law that allow for $250,000 per person ($500,000 for a married couple) tax-free in net gains from appreciation when you sell (if your home has been lived in for an aggregate of two out of the previous five years) also encourages fluidity of homeownership and reinforces viewing your home as an investment—perhaps the best one you can possibly make.

The third item in Pollan's plan is never to retire. Since people are living longer, he maintains (and I agree) that it no longer makes sense to arbitrarily think that a certain age, like 65, means you should stop working. He questions the notion that retirement is necessarily more fulfilling than staying productive with work.

Psychologists would agree with him that it is desirable for seniors to be involved in meaningful work, which keeps them feeling purposeful and appreciated, and improves their physical and emotional health. And, of course, he is thinking that continued productivity will also mean a continued stream of income, even if it is reduced compared to one's earlier earning capacity.

The final item of Pollan's plan is the most relevant for our purposes, and that is to "die broke." But by this he does not mean to die a penniless pauper—it's just a catchy way to say that you should look at inheritance in a different vein. And it specifically means having no assets that may be taxed at the end of your life.

Pollan submits that during a past era when inheritance consisted mostly of fixed assets, inheritance was a more viable concept than it is today. He uses the example of a family farm or a business being the basis for a contract between generations. A son might work the farm to help support his parents in exchange for receiving the farm from Dad when he dies. Pollan asserts this family contract is no longer valid.

Pollan further believes that "creating and making an estate does nothing but damage the person doing the hoarding. It will force you to put the quality of your death before the quality of your life" (pp. 14–15). He argues that assets we would put into a trust should be used while we are alive, that we should give gifts to our family members to help them at varying periods of their lives, rather than hording them until we die and then given to financially established children who may not need help as much as they did earlier in their lives. To some degree, this is an appealing argument when combined with his touching on a couple of the emotional issues that are created by the traditional system of inheritance.

For example, estates and potential inheritances may encourage children to become greedy, resulting in the trustor parent never being sure of her children's motives. Does the child come and take care of me because he has one eye on maintaining his share of the inheritance? Or because he loves me and cares about me? The parent is put in the position of having to deal with these kinds of questions.

Because the family contract of inheritance is no longer as valid as it used to be, Pollan sees inheritance as "soul killing," in that a child has to wait for a parent to die before he is able to come into his own, rather than earn it himself. It encourages the mistaken belief, Pollan says, that money has an intrinsic value in itself, rather than just being a tool to satisfy human needs. While the use of the term "soul killing" seems overstated, it's true that some studies indicate that trust fund children are not as motivated as children who don't know they have a large inheritance coming later in life. As an alternative way of viewing the disposition of assets, Pollan's thinking adds something of value to the discussion. And it encourages children to stop believing inheritance is their birthright.

CHAPTER 7
DECIDING TO PLAN FOR YOU
AND YOUR CLAN

If you go the conventional route, you will want to do some estate planning for yourself and your family. Even if you choose to spend or give away much of your assets in the form of gifts before you die, it's still important to have an estate plan in place to handle as many of the contingencies that may arise as possible. This chapter will briefly identify some of the basics of estate planning, including some of the psychological issues arising in doing this planning.*

After gathering information from various sources, consult an attorney. Make sure to seek out one who specializes in estate planning when you are ready to draw up the various legal documents. Unlike preparing your taxes, this is one of those areas of the law that you really don't want to tackle on your own. You will need help, as addressing your own particular needs requires an expert who can tailor your plan to your unique situation. An estate attorney can make sure it is done correctly for it to be thorough, of lasting value, and valid in court.

Keep in mind that you can expect to feel anything ranging from a mild to a strong avoidance of doing this planning. You will notice wanting to avoid even *thinking* about it, as doing so forces us to face our own death and to make decisions about how we want our assets distributed. Because of this resistance, you will find it easy to procrastinate. One form of this procrastination will be to tell yourself that you're "too young" and

---

*Be sure to consult the online links given in the reference section at the end of this book for more in-depth material on the legal aspects of estate planning. An easy-to-read legal book that appreciates the emotional side of inheritance is *Beyond the Grave* by Gerald M. Condon and Jeffrey L. Condon, noted in the references.

don't really need to worry about an estate plan in general and an inheritance plan in particular. One powerful way to help prevent potential inheritance blood wars is to resist this excuse making as it comes up and *decide to plan*. Then follow through with your decision—and do it sooner rather than later. Do it by the time you reach age 45, if not earlier— especially if you've built a solid financial foundation before this age, have children, work in a physically risky or highly stressful occupation, or have special medical problems that could be life threatening.

We must accept that the world we live in today has increased personal risk. Besides accident and illness, outside forces (such as terrorist attacks) may end our lives without much warning. Especially if you are married and have children, it is important to protect your wealth and to make sure, in case of sudden death, your assets end up where you want them to—not left in the hands of a probate judge.

Even though estate planning requires some tough choices, it is important for your peace of mind—and the peace of mind of your partner— to make them. Of course, you will have to update your plan as time goes by should you change your mind about any of your choices or as family circumstances change. But the important thing is to decide to have a plan and then to follow through with it rather than procrastinate.

WHAT IS AN ESTATE PLAN?

The broad basic components of estate planning include:

- *Wills and trusts*. These are the most important tools for protecting your family and assets. At the least, you want a will; there are some strong advantages to having a revocable living trust, explained below.
- *Advance health-care directives*. An important part of a will or trust that allows you to designate someone to make medical and legal decisions for you in case you are unable to communicate your own wishes.
- *Life insurance*. How much or even having life insurance depends on your family situation and your other net assets and their ability to care

for your family. It is not considered absolutely necessary for everyone, and many financial planners consider it to be a poor investment. But it has traditionally been viewed as an element of planning.

- *Financial planning.* This includes managing your finances to make sure you have adequate assets to meet your needs during retirement and making sure the person you want receives the proceeds from your investment vehicles. It also includes the use of a power of attorney document, authorizing someone to act on your behalf if you are unable to do it yourself. In addition, it may include the use of temporary or permanent guardianships or conservatorships if you are unable to make decisions yourself.

  This category also has to do with the actual forms of investment retirement plans, such as IRAs, Keoghs, and 401(k)s, and the types of investments that may be made in each of them. It's to your advantage to have more than just a passing interest in where you money is invested. If we have learned anything from the severe bear market years, it's that we can no longer afford *not* to pay close attention to how our savings and retirement assets are invested. We must be willing to learn the basics of various investment vehicles and not be afraid to actively participate in the management of these investments. At the very least, we need to be closely watching over the investments a financial planner or brokerage fund manager makes on our behalf.

- *Housing alternatives.* This includes thinking about all the considerations relevant to where you want to live as you grow older, including cost, independence, care, accessibility, safety, and social relationships. Options may include living at home, with or without in-home assistance, and outside care facilities and retirement communities. If you draw up your trust when you are in your 40s or 50s, this item may seem irrelevant for some time to come. Some in this age range, however, are already signing up for assisted-living insurance to make it cheaper over the years. Most likely you will discuss housing with your family as it becomes necessary.

Because many of you will already have in place some financial planning (through life insurance, savings, retirement accounts, and other investing vehicles), your primary task is to go ahead and draw up a will or living trust along with health-care directives to complete an estate plan.

DIFFERENCES BETWEEN A WILL AND A LIVING TRUST

Both wills and trusts are legal instruments you can use to dictate how your estate will be dealt with upon your death. If you can afford to hire an estate attorney to set up a living trust, I highly recommend it. I've had one in effect for a number of years and believe it is well worth the money spent for the long-term advantages gained. From the perspective of both having my own family trust as well as dealing with my mother's trust after her death, I've seen the clear advantages of a living trust.

However, if you're single, don't have a lot of assets, and don't want to spend the money to hire an attorney to set up a trust, just have an attorney help you draw up a will and then have him review it. Let's contrast some of the basics.

A will allows you to have the last word after your death, dictating who will receive your property. You choose who will carry out your wishes, as well as other important decisions, like who you want to care for your minor children, if you have any. There are specific formalities in the signing of a will that you must follow for it to hold up in court, should it be contested.

Some details in drawing up a will are significant if you don't deal with them but are not things you would normally consider. For example, if you choose to write your will out in longhand, it must not be done on any kind of paper that has a logo or imprinted name and address. It must be plain or lined paper. This is why it is important to have the help of an attorney, or at least read up on requirements to make sure you do everything according to the legal requirements where you live. (See the online references at the end of the book for sources to find an attorney in your area.) You can always make changes to the will after you sign it, unless the changes are substantial. Then it is best to sign a new will, which revokes the earlier one.

One variation of a will is called a pour-over will, used in conjunction with a living trust. This enables whatever remaining assets are outside of a trust to be put into it and then distributed to your beneficiaries. This type of will is usually done at the same time as a living trust.

One of the main differences between a will and a living trust is that a will is subject to probate proceedings, while a living trust is not. Probate is the court-supervised legal process that includes determining the validity of your will, gathering your assets, paying debts and taxes, and distributing the remaining assets to those entitled to them. This process can be costly and time consuming, especially if anyone decides to challenge the will. In addition, a will becomes public record at the time of your death, while a trust remains private. Most people don't like the idea that when a parent dies, their family assets may be open to public inspection and outside challenge.

What a living trust allows you to do is have property transferred after you die through your "out of the grave" agent, either a child or another appointed trustee. Rather than have a judge deal with transferring property, you can have your agent do it privately and without the costs of probate. In effect, a trust allows you to have your name signed so that all property may be transferred as you wish—but only after you die. As long as you are alive, you continue to be in full control of your trust and can change it in any way you wish. This is why they call it a "revocable" trust.

With a will, you must use a power of attorney or conservatorship to manage your assets, which isn't required with a living trust. For most people, it's wise to spend the extra money to set up a living trust, knowing you will get back this cost when it's time to distribute your assets through not having to pay the probate costs that go with a will. The flexibility and privacy of a living trust make it appealing.

CHOOSING A SUCCESSOR TRUSTEE

One of the interesting psychological questions faced when setting up a living trust is who will be designated as your "successor trustee," or the person who will be given broad powers to make decisions and interpret your stated wishes. This person is ultimately responsible for signing to transfer your property and handle your affairs. The powers entrusted to this person are far-reaching, so it's important that the person be honest, trustworthy, and competent.

Some attorneys believe that it's best to name all of your children as successor co-trustees. This allows all of them to be involved in the trust administration. Gerald Condon and Jeffrey Condon, in their book *Beyond the Grave*, hold this view, believing that a child can choose not to participate if he or she wishes, but that it's best to let each decide so that he or she doesn't end up feeling the parent favored one child over the others. These attorneys maintain that the possible compounding of the complexity of administrating the estate will be countered by the mutual desire for all children to agree on issues so that they may see the inheritance. Because cooperating with each other will mean all get their money sooner, they believe co-trustees will be motivated to speed up the process.

Now, if you think about it, this is a curious position for estate attorneys to take. They are well aware of how strong emotions and power struggles come into play—being on the front line of the blood wars, they see it all the time. I don't agree that the desire to speed up the process so that all may reap their inheritance more quickly is a stronger motivation than the need to attempt to exert one's personal control over the situation.

As a psychologist, I see the choice of co-trustees rather than a single trustee as more likely to set up a predicament of unending argument and disagreement, bickering, and the eruption of power struggles. What I have seen in my own family in dealing with my mother's estate is that no small or large decisions would have been easily made if all three brothers needed to agree on each and every decision.

Because we would have all had a right to be consulted on every decision if we were co-executors, it would have been difficult to simply put a portion of the decision making in one sibling's hands to take care of practical matters. Each time we "gave away" a portion of decision making, it would feel like giving away a part of our control.

It seems easier to appoint a single executor, and then have this person *consult and seriously consider* the opinions of the other siblings on relevant matters so they felt involved in the process. Much of the practical, detail-oriented tasks don't require more than one competent person to handle. Too many details need to be attended to, and requiring all children to agree on all decision making can easily grind the process to a halt.

Parents should inform their heirs as to whom they have chosen to be their executor. If they choose one of their children, this child may then make his or her job easier by gathering information about the location of important documents, such as the will, bank accounts, safe-deposit boxes, and loans. Another advantage of this disclosure is that the other children know ahead of time and can express their reactions to the parent directly. If an outsider is chosen as executor, it's good for the children to have this information as well.

Here is an admittedly extreme example of the inheritance process grinding to a halt. Whether it be from simple ignorance, incompetence, or manipulative passivity, it shows what can happen when siblings are unable to do what seems to be obvious to move the process forward.

Martha dies in 1996. She leaves her house to her five children. One of the children, Gina, was named executor of the will but didn't do anything to settle the estate. So the other sibs voted to remove her. One of the brothers, John, was voted to take over as executor. But he also did nothing to settle the will.

All five brothers and sisters discussed whether to sell or rent their mother's house but couldn't agree what to do. As they procrastinated over seven years, John continued to pay property taxes, but he did nothing else to bring the decision making to a head. John then told his siblings that he was "waiting to take the house away from them." One sibling wonders whether he can legally get away with this and says that the rest of the sibs don't have much money to spend on hiring an attorney.

You would think that adult sibs could figure out that waiting seven years to settle an estate is a big mistake! But here we have four sibs, all of whom sit back passively and allow a fifth sib to do nothing *for seven years*, with hopes of the house becoming his by what is called "adverse possession." Both federal and state laws exist that allow a person to gain title to land from the actual owner simply by using the land out in the open for all to see. The idea is that an owner who does not dispute the user's right over a certain period may lose rights to the property. However, the typical rules don't apply to an estate, so the son's plan of gaining it by holding it for a specific period won't work.

But the main point here is how emotional and psychological issues among sibs can create a situation whereby no one takes the expected action to make sure a probate judge decides how to handle the house. We can only explain this passivity for such an extraordinarily long time with a psychological interpretation. And that is that all sibs are fearful of confronting the one who is abusing his elected role as executor.

To think that siblings will act rationally during their grieving and agree to one child handling some decisions without their approval is, I believe, wishful thinking. While it may be possible in some families, I don't think it's something that we can expect. And that's just the issue of handling all the practical details that must be attended to when a parent dies. The real problems lie in the struggles that ensue from siblings' fears of being controlled and treated unfairly by the others.

As I have emphasized, after the death of a parent—and especially the second parent—all past sibling resentments and psychological dynamics come into play. In addition, for a period of months we may feel confused and "spaced out." Those close to the parent, especially children, get lost in dealing with the internal images, memories, recent conversations, and emotions in trying to comprehend and cope with the loss.

Important decisions should not be made until we have had a chance to recover from this numbing process that is part of grieving. The reason for this is that emotion is likely to overwhelm clear, rational thinking. At the very least, it's a good idea to consult a trusted spouse or friend if you are forced to make any decisions in the first two or three months that can't be undone. We'll come back to this numbing/confusion in a later chapter on grieving.

Condon and Condon qualify their suggestion for appointing co-trustees by saying that when there is a history of sibling rivalry, it may not be such a good idea to appoint co-trustees. That may seem like good advice, but *all* families have a history of sibling rivalry!

If that rivalry is not obvious on the surface, then it's just a matter of scratching that surface to find it. The death of a parent, especially the final parent, is the scratching of the surface that allows these issues to bubble up. These dynamics are going to come into play *whether or not siblings are even aware of them.*

From my own experience in watching what happened in my family, it seems far more likely that the combination of these sibling dynamics and the mental confusion that accompanies grieving lead to power struggles rather than to cooperation. So I can't agree with attorneys who, as a general guideline, think parents are doing the right thing by naming all of their children co-trustees.

Making any simple generalizations is too difficult. Whether sisters will cooperate more easily than brothers or whether those who are further apart in age will have an easier time than those who are closer in age is impossible to know. Nor can we say that those in their 50s will be more rational than those in their 30s or 40s, or that those sibs who live geographically closer to one another will be any more or less cooperative than those who live at a distance.

Many variables are at work in each unique family constellation, affecting how the emotional process of inheritance plays itself out. That is why we need to be careful about making generalizations that will prove to be untrue.

Because it's more difficult (but still possible) for siblings or other family members to challenge the trustor's distribution wishes in a living trust compared to a will, the broad powers granted the trustee mean that there is potential for abuse and favoritism. The trustee who is a sibling rather than an outside appointed attorney or accountant, for example,

may consciously or unconsciously make policy decisions that favor him-
or herself. He may play two other sibs against each other, or create family
alliances that unconsciously repeat earlier patterns in the relationships.

Because one responsibility is controlling funds to pay the temporary
costs of the estate, the sib in control may abuse the responsibility by
shifting some of the trust funds to personal accounts. It would be difficult for other family members to be aware of or easily trace this kind of
action. Because of this, a responsible trustee will make sure sibs are
given an ongoing accounting of assets and that all their questions are answered about how estate expenses are being paid.

Parents need to know that no matter how well their trust documents
are drawn up, the successor trustee does not have to follow them exactly
as instructed. Again, in naming this trustee, you are granting broad powers that are always subject to interpretation. So in choosing a successor
trustee, you want someone who has shown good judgment in the past
and who you reasonably believe will follow your instructions—both the
specifics and the spirit of them, when interpretation is necessary.

Sibs should remember that power struggles may likely arise during
the inheritance process—that doesn't have to mean you can't agree on
specific decisions that need to be made. Things may get slowed down
for a while when there is an impasse. Communications may either become intense or break down altogether. A flurry of phone calls, faxes,
and e-mails may occupy a great deal of your time and attention. And
they may mean poor sleep, worry, and ugly feelings toward your sibs.
But everyone's desire to see a resolution to the process for their own gain
does tend to push the process along in all but the ugliest of cases.

Psychologically, what is important is not primarily whether sibling
rivalries will be played out (assume they will) as much as the need to
trust and accept the final decisions the executor makes. When this basic
trust is not in place, the odds go up of significant problems leading to extended and aggravated legal actions. And that becomes the stuff of
blood wars and nightmares.

If parents don't believe their children have a basic trust among
themselves that the chosen sib is going to be as fair as possible to all

parties concerned, it's best for parents to consider appointing an outside, independent trustee. While this will cost the trust money that would not otherwise have to be spent if the role was filled by a child, it may be worth it if sibling relationships have not been founded on and fortified by a sufficient level of trust.

To prevent potential problems, parents contemplating a successor trustee seriously need to consider whether their other children have this kind of trust in whichever child they select to play this role. And because your parents may ask you for your opinion on who to choose, you need to think about how much you trust your sibs.

ASSESSING YOUR LEVEL OF CHILD/SIBLING TRUST

Just as I asked you to consider your feelings of entitlement, now I want you to think about your feelings of trust in your children/sibs. These questions regarding trust are meant for both parents making the choice of a successor trustee and for siblings in asssessing the potential for problems.

1. Do you have confidence in the education and common sense of each of your children/sibs to make clear, rational decsions in handling basic business affairs?

2. Do you trust that each of your sibs can take care of such practical issues as closing credit card accounts, handling bills that need to be paid, keeping other family members apprised in writing of a chronology of estate events, selling estate items, if necessary, and all the other administrative issues that will arise?

3. Do you trust that when it comes time to consider a system for the distribution of personal property, each of your siblings will ask for and seriously consider your input?

4. Do you trust that each of your sibs is committed enough to fairness and equality and understand the psychological dynamics involved in inheritance that they would read relevant literature before beginning the process?

5. Does your past experience with each of your sibs indicate their ability to keep good records, manage their own business affairs, and handle in a timely and competent manner their basic finances and investments?

6. Is the person being considered for trustee able to overcome the emotions of loss and grieving enough to handle the affairs of the estate? This is an important question, as the grieving process may enter into decision making more than you think. How have they handled any past losses? Did they have any "unfinished business" of an emotional nature that might grossly interfere with making basic decisions?

Not having this basic level of confidence and trust in the ability of your sibs is an indication of potential problems. It may suggest that all involved consider using an outside attorney to act as executor, even if one of the sibs has been appointed. (Of course, getting the chosen sib to give up control is another matter.) Or it may simply signal a specific area that needs to be addressed, such as an agreement to comanage the finances of the estate or obtain the services of an outside consultant, such as an attorney or accountant.

What's important here is not that each sibling have legal knowledge. (But if you have an attorney in the family or know one outside the family you trust, they should be seriously given the advantage by a parent deciding who to choose.) What matters is that you have the trust and confidence that whoever is acting as trustee has the ability to utilize outside expertise to help in decision making, as needed.

Remember, one benefit of a living trust is its flexibility; it allows for a successor trustee to refuse to play the part for any reason he or she chooses. Some children and spouses simply are not prepared to take on the tasks required, since the commitment of time and effort (when they likely will not be paid anything for their services) is more than they are willing to expend. Some don't want to expose themselves to the aggravation of potential conflicts with their sibs. And some just don't feel they can handle the challenges when they are still trying to grieve the loss of their parent. When you are drawing up your trust papers and have to decide on a successor trustee, consider all these factors.

When parents and children can talk openly about their estate plans, this is exactly the kind of issue that can be discussed, so that everyone's feelings are considered.

PLANNING FOR THE "WHAT IF" CONTINGENCY

One of the challenging aspects of constructing a living trust is being forced to consider various scenarios, all of which are undesirable and some of which may be your worst nightmare. Doing this "what if" thinking may bring up anticipatory anxiety and fears of loss. Because the living trust is attempting to cover all possible scenarios regarding you and your family's future, you are asked to think about contingencies that you may never before have had to consider. Nobody wants to think about the possibility that you and everyone you care for could all get wiped out in a tragedy. But that's exactly what your attorney will force you to consider in coming up with a contingency plan of succession.

For example, let's say you're married and have a couple of kids. Your attorney will ask you to think about who you would like your money to go to if you die but your spouse lives on. Easy—you give it to your spouse. But who do you choose if your spouse happens to die with you? Let's say you both have the bad luck to die in a plane crash. If your children are still minors, you must decide who would be the one you want to care for them and whether this person is the one you want to take control of your assets. Your trust can be set up so that your money is portioned out for your kids' needs, and they only have a legal right to the funds directly when they reach a designated age.

But let's say you have in mind a sibling to take custody of your children. The attorney will then ask you a "what if" question like this: "What if your two brothers happen to be in the airplane with you and you all plunge to your deaths? Who's next in line that you would like to take care of your kids and be in control of your estate?"

Let's say you tell him next in line would be an aunt, and then a good friend. He then asks, "What if the aunt and good friend both refuse to take your children or to be executor of your estate?" You can see how the "what if?" process works here. You're forced to think a number of levels down from what you would normally think about when it comes to possible disaster contingency plans.

You'll be asked to specify exactly how much (either an absolute dollar amount or percentage) you wish to leave each person or institution. If, over time, your thinking changes, you can always change these amounts. Going through this exercise is the best way to be forced to think very thoroughly about how you want your estate to be divided. This "what if?" contingency planning—not to mention having to contemplate their own death—scares people and pushes them into procrastination.

You will also be asked to create a separate list if you have personal possessions you want to go to specific friends or family members. One of the side effects of thinking about who you want to have your personal possessions is that you realize which objects are of real monetary value and which are important to you but really more of sentimental value. You may also begin to think about giving away some of these objects long before you ever are faced with disease or death. To help deal with the contingencies of disease or being mentally unable to make decisions, more documents are drawn up to help follow your wishes.

LEGAL AND HEALTH-CARE DIRECTIVES

What is called the "power of attorney" is a document that authorizes someone else to act on your behalf in a number of situations, such as in a business, real estate, or health-care decision. The person you appoint is called an "agent" or "attorney-in-fact." The power of attorney can authorize the attorney-in-fact to perform a single or a number of acts repeatedly.

The power of attorney is revoked if you become incapacitated unless you include a provision allowing it to stay in effect. For you to have your agent continue to make decisions on your behalf if you're incapacitated, you must include wording that makes the power of attorney "durable." Then the agent continues to have the power to make decisions when you become incapacitated.

The durable power of attorney is part of the package that you sign when you design a living trust. What is called a "durable power of attorney for health care" specifically relates to decisions pertaining to your health. It may be invoked in decisions regarding your wish to receive life-sustaining procedures in case you become permanently comatose or terminally ill. It may also be applied to such issues as whether you need to be placed in a convalescent care facility or should stay at home with nursing care.

For example, my mother had signed a durable power of attorney on admitting her for health care. When she had a brief hospitalization, as standard procedure, the hospital staff asked her if she wished to be revived if her pulse stopped and she went into a coma. Because the doctor was considering an exploratory procedure that could cause this to occur, he needed to know her wishes.

She told him that, yes, she wanted to be kept alive as long as there was any chance that she could be revived. Since she was still quite competent, the durable power of attorney didn't come into play. You can imagine how hard it is to sit and listen to this kind of discussion—both for my mother as a patient and for me as her son. The durable power of attorney for health care stated that any two of the three brothers needed to agree if "extraordinary" measures were to be used to keep her alive.

During the middle of one night in the hospital, in her frustration, disorientation from various medications, and being in a strange place, my mother said to a nurse that she did not want any further dialysis performed. She was not instructing the nurses to keep from caring for her, just expressing her fatigue from being poked, lifted, and not exactly given the most sensitive of care. Her body was weak, and because her skin had become thin, she bruised easily. She had been forced to be hooked up to numerous tubes and sit through countless hours of dialysis. And she didn't like the treatment given by one particular aide, who she believed in some way violated her personal dignity.

The next morning the nurse reported to me that my mother said she didn't want to live. In addition, just before I arrived in the morning my mother had told the dialysis nurse she didn't want to be hooked up. At this point—besides expecting the nurses to understand that they must go ahead and give the treatment and not listen to a comment made in frustration—I was able to use the "clout" of the power of attorney for health care and make sure they went ahead and gave her the dialysis treatment. While she had not at all been judged as incompetent to make her own decisions, the fact that I was listed as one of the agents with power of attorney made the nurses listen to me more authoritatively. In fact, this document is considered important enough that its existence is noted in the patient's file.

But this incident raised an issue that I brought up when, a couple of days later, my mother was back home and feeling better. I told her what had happened and that we needed to know under what conditions she wanted us to let her die or whether she still wanted all measures taken to keep her alive. Even though we were already aware of her general wishes, I wanted to hear her say them again, as a result of the incident in the hospital. The issue is this: Even though these wishes can be written out, they still need to be interpreted. And it is obviously best for them to be interpreted by those closest to her—not by an absentee doctor or impersonal nurses.

One of my brothers was there, as was my wife. We all needed to hear what she wanted, given the mental confusion and frustration that any patient can experience in the hospital. Though quite brief, this had been her first emergency hospitalization since dealing with her blood cancer. My mother made it clear she wanted any and all measures taken to keep her alive, unless she was clearly not going to come out of a coma. She also made it clear that we were not to listen to any of her rantings of frustration in the moment to let her die, should this happen again.

While I was relieved to hear her feelings, this wasn't an easy conversation to initiate—even for me, whose psychotherapy work requires that I be able to initiate conversations about anything with anybody. But it was necessary. Should the situation arise again, I didn't want to misinterpret her wishes because of a moment of my anxiety or her exasperation. Interestingly enough, my mother *did not even recall* telling the nurse she wanted to die, although she did recall being handled roughly and wanting to get out of the hospital as soon as possible.

While everyone involved takes the power of attorney for health care seriously, I need to mention that some attorneys are not confident that the general power of attorney document will stand up should you want to use it to gain access to your parent's bank accounts or brokerage accounts, while he or she is still alive.

Because the general power of attorney is valid only when your parent is mentally incapacitated or incompetent, these institutions are circumspect about taking your word that your parent has actually been certified as such. They may not trust that your parent's signature is valid, or that your parent was actually capable and competent when the document was signed. They may simply refuse to honor the document, no matter how much you protest or try to convince them that it is valid.

It may then be necessary for a child to get a document that the financial institutions will accept as a court order, such as a conservatorship. Getting a conservatorship is itself a drawn-out process, because it permits the person in question to make a case before a judge that he or she is of sound mind. But if you have a living trust, you don't need this conservatorship, because a special provision in the trust will allow a child or children to take over as trustee to make decisions—if they have been added to the document previously.

Here is a simple example of the kind of resistance you may encounter using the durable power of attorney when you haven't been added to the trust account in question. I wanted to be put on my mother's brokerage account, which was in her trust, so that I could make some stock sales quickly through her broker. I was following the market closely, and my mother wanted me to be able to sell some stocks when I believed the time was right. She didn't want to be bothered making the call herself, as she was coping with her poor health.

Although her brokerage company sent me copies of her monthly statements, they would not legally add me to her trust account to enable me to transact trades. They were told by their legal department that I needed to have a letter from her trust attorney giving me permission.

Because my mother didn't have an attorney at the time and most of our attention was devoted to her medical condition, we ended up not following through.

However, I circumvented the legal issue, making the sales (with my mother's permission) directly with her broker, with whom we had a long-term relationship. But the point is, when it comes to trusts and legal documents, institutions are taught to err on the side of caution. For the trustor, this is a positive, as it helps protect him or her from scheming children or others. For the child trying to help with decision making, it's not so good. But this is one of the safety mechanisms built into a trust.

EXPRESSING YOUR WISHES IN YOUR WILL

Whether or not you ultimately choose to discuss your preferences for the distribution of your personal possessions with your children, if you don't want problems to arise with your executor and children, it's important to use the will as the place to state your intentions. One of the themes of this book is that blood wars are the result of poor (or no) communication between parents and children when it comes to what I have termed "the inheritance taboo." To lessen the likelihood of blood wars erupting, the very least a parent should do is take advantage of the will as the place where sentimental or valuable personal items will be listed and your preference of who receives them will be clearly stated.

The common result of not using a will to list preferences regarding important possessions is misunderstanding among children. Disagreements begin when more than one child believes the same item was "supposed to be" given or had been "promised" to her. Because the children believe that their parent wanted them to have a certain item, it is easy for arguments to take place over what *he or she* desires, rather than what the parent actually might have intended. When you clearly write out and state your preferences, you make this whole area of potential dispute much more manageable.

Your trust attorney will suggest you add this list at the back of your will, as well as a sheet listing your separate property from your spouse. But most attorneys are not going to push this issue, so it's something that you have to be thinking about yourself when you have your trust and will drawn up. Of course, you can add this anytime later, if you choose.

The problem is that for the majority of us, simply dealing with all of the choices involved in creating the trust or will is all we want to face at the time. We don't want to detail who gets what possessions because, unless we are in the process of dying, we don't think it's necessary. This is the kind of thing that we often forget until years later when it becomes more relevant. And the ambivalence we have about facing this issue may be played out by not *ever* coming back to the will to itemize our wishes.

At the very least, when you have your trust or will drawn up, think about any possessions that you know you want to be given to someone in particular. If, when you think about it, *you can't bear the thought of anyone else getting that item* because you haven't made it clear, then take the time to list it in your will so that you won't have to think about it later. The two obvious categories to consider here are valuable jewelry and sentimental family heirlooms. These are the two groups of items (besides money and real estate) that easily create the most potential friction between children when no clear determination has been made as to their disposition.

This chapter has briefly identified the basic components of estate planning and made the case that you simply can't afford to build up assets over a lifetime without taking legal precautions to protect them. In the same way people need to have various types of insurance to protect themselves, the task of doing estate planning is vital to your family's welfare. No one needs to be convinced to obtain home, health, or auto insurance. But because estate planning means having to make tough decisions about what happens to your assets when you die, it becomes easy to avoid until it may be too late.

This chapter completes Part One, which should ideally be read *well before* a family health or legal crisis occurs. When inheritance issues are not part of your present reality, you can consider them deliberately and carefully. This makes for more rational decision making and allows plenty of time to discuss with your family the various options before everyone is thrown into the frenzy of crisis.

But because the inheritance taboo is so powerful and the personal resistances so strong, large numbers will simply refuse to deal with these issues before absolutely necessary. While a will or trust may be in place, it's the more personal and emotional issues that you will avoid.

With this in mind, in Part Two we will delve into the issues that arise when we are facing a family crisis and dealing with the death of a parent. For those wanting information to tackle these problems *before* they occur, reading the following chapters will act as a window into what you will be facing if you refuse to do any planning or refuse to verbalize your preferences to your children. Once you've overcome your resistance and made the decision to do estate and inheritance planning, the legal aspects of inheritance aren't so challenging, but the emotional issues are.

PART TWO:
DURING CRISIS
AND AFTER DEATH

CHAPTER 8
EXPLORING BELIEFS, VALUES, AND EMOTIONS

Let's assume you've picked up this book during a crisis. We will consider a crisis to include (but not be limited to) any of the following:

- A legal or emotional issue involving inheritance is facing you or your family—you are unsure how to cope with it, and it is creating stress in your life.
- Adult children are trying to get a parent to face the fact that he or she is incapacitated and/or dying and needs to make his or her final wishes for inheritance known.
- A parent or other family member has had a life-threatening accident, is acutely ill, or has a progressive illness, and there is reason to believe he or she will die from it.
- Family members are feeling anxious about a parent who has gradually demonstrated signs of physical or mental deterioration.
- Through some dramatic incident, a parent has shown the marked inability to use good judgment in decision making regarding self-care, finances, etc., and there is need for family intervention.
- A family member is in critical condition, ready to die, or has died.

Let's further assume you are picking up this book in hopes of finding ways to cope with the emotional and psychological issues that are part of your family crisis. You want to find ways to deal with the emotions of the inheritance taboo, gain insight into your own reactions and the reactions of family members, comply with your parent's inheritance wishes, and save yourself and your siblings from engaging in destructive blood wars.

We will make one more assumption: By "crisis" we don't necessarily mean being on one's deathbed. A crisis may last months or even years, in the case of a progressively deteriorating medical condition.

Those are the assumptions we will make as we begin Part Two of this book.

As a qualifier to what follows, consider that one of the reasons a book like this has never been written before is that it's difficult to give very specific "cookbook"-type recipes when each individual and family constellation is different. Their particular psychological dynamics are different, and the various permutations of inheritance drama players and situations are different.

> **[!]** Because of this, I will as much as possible try to escape the traps of the typical prescriptive mode of self-help books. The real value of this book is not in giving you overly simplistic solutions to complicated situations but in helping you enhance your awareness of how your *own role* in the family and your *unresolved issues* with sibs will affect their reactions in dealing with inheritance. At the same time, I'll give you suggestions about certain general tools that will facilitate this process, no matter what the particulars of your situation may be.

Let's begin by reiterating the basic family conspiracy—built deeply into the culture—to preserve the inheritance taboo. I include in the taboo not just dealing with who gets what possessions, but the psychological task of gaining as much closure between parent and children as possible before the parent dies.

THE LEVELS OF DENIAL

During a family crisis, the taboo against talking about inheritance will be buttressed by the powerful resistance you and your family will experience by utilizing denial. The defense mechanisms of denial and rationalization (excuse making) may take the form of misjudging the seriousness of the crisis itself and pushing away the possible outcome of death.

> **!** Some forms of denial will be more transparent, while others will be more subtle and indirect. All, however, will be aimed at pretending that *what you know, intuit, or believe to be happening at one level isn't really happening at all.* And this denial will be operating both consciously and unconsciously.

Even if your parent has seen fit to do estate planning and discuss basics with family members, it's often very difficult to face a deteriorating medical condition and the process of dying by talking about it openly with loved ones. The worse the physical and mental conditions become, for some, the more difficult it is to face or talk about. For others, obsessing about the details of the medical condition will help them avoid talking about dying and their inheritance wishes. So the first level of denial we'll see is in the parent who is facing the crisis.

One form of this first-level denial in the earlier stages of a crisis is the parent not considering his or her own condition serious. It may also take the form of strong resistance to proposed interventions by healthcare providers or family to curtail any of the parent's freedoms.

For example, some parents don't want to admit that they can no longer see well enough to drive at night. They may not want to use a hearing aid or give up their driver's license when their reactions are no longer fast enough for them to drive safely. They may refuse to consider having help doing everyday tasks.

Numerous other large and small restrictions of freedom will be resisted, such as admitting they can no longer live on their own without assistance or are unable to manage their finances. One of the toughest things for some is to admit that they are no longer thinking clearly, resulting in bad judgment and poor decisions. This is especially tough because they may not even notice that they are not thinking rationally and because we tend to put more emphasis on the loss of mental faculties than we do on the deterioration or breakdown of the body.

The parent may experience these behaviors as the healthy exerting of his independent spirit and try to maintain his personal dignity to care for himself. Initially, this resistance to admitting weakness and needing help may also serve to stave off fear, anxiety, and depression. The sick person does not want to overly alarm family members or ask for too much help. But often what they are doing is denying real limitations that, unacknowledged and disrespected, will only tend to increase the chances of accident or injury.

The second level of denial occurs in those spouses who are unable to cope with the illness or crisis of their partner. Some will forbid you from mentioning anything directly to the sick or dying parent about their condition. Because they have not come to grips with the severity of the condition, they can't tolerate anyone else dealing with the issue more directly.

When a spouse is able to accept what's going on, supporting and facilitating open communication, she can pave the way for more direct communication with the suffering parent. If the parent is unable to tolerate speaking too directly about dying or his inheritance wishes, the spouse may act as a conduit who can reach her partner when no one else may be emotionally allowed in.

The third level of denial may be in the children, who also will tend to diminish the seriousness of the illness and procrastinate in dealing with decision making for the parent in question, especially when there is no spouse involved. They may grant the sick person much more ability to think clearly than he or she is capable of because they can't bear to accept that their mother or father is no longer strong and able. They don't want to have to begin the process of switching roles, wherein the children slowly become caregivers to the parent. To accept this need for a switch in roles means to accept they'll never again be nurtured by the parent in the same way as they always have been.

When we see children putting off making important decisions regarding the caretaking of their parent, for example, we can often trace it to an ambivalence leading to this procrastination. One part of the child wants to make the decision and get someone to assist the parent, but another part of him doesn't want to offend the parent or be too quick to limit his freedom. A child may avoid making numerous decisions over the course of an illness that drags out for months or years as a result of this kind of ambivalence, denial, and procrastination.

Typically, it may take a dramatic unfortunate accident to wake up all children that the parent is simply no longer able to handle a specific freedom and needs much more care. Suddenly, then, children are forced to realize the need for shifting their thinking because their parent is no longer functioning well.

Health-care providers constitute the fourth level of denial. It is easy to want to pretend your parent isn't really so ill or dying as long as doctors, nurses, and other health-care providers continue to tell you to "have hope" or "think positively," or hold out the possibility of a medical cure. As we said in Chapter 1, thinking positively is great when, caught in the early stages, you have to put up a fight with a disease like cancer or being diagnosed HIV-positive.

Doing everything possible to fight your disease is fine, and your efforts can truly make a difference. But I'm talking now about the time to accept *what is*, to accept that your parent is losing his physical and/or mental abilities and needs help. Or to accept that despite whatever course of treatment, your parent is dying. And it is because we are usually not quite sure how long the parent has to live that it is easy to rationalize never facing death.

Doctors participate in the conspiracy of silence around death and dying when they won't tell you the truth until it is too late but will continue to try various medical procedures, operations, and medicines right up until the time you die. It is part of their training and oath of practice to give people hope, trying their best to keep them alive and out of as much pain as possible, no matter how close to death they may be. Even when nothing more can be done by medical science, many physicians will not talk openly about death to a patient unless the patient brings it up first. And then some will not be entirely truthful.

Sometimes this denial is what the patient needs, such as when the pain of facing the end of one's life is intolerable. But too often, it works to keep people from facing their own death and dealing more openly and directly with related issues, such as inheritance wishes and other business affairs and saying final good-byes to loved ones.

A fifth level of denial may be seen in extended family and friends, who are at times too quick to try to make the ill person in question feel good by distracting him from his condition because they, too, are so uncomfortable in dealing with dying that they just can't bring up the subject. *When all of these levels are working together, we have a strong conspiracy of silence.*

> **!** As a psychologist, I'm astonished to see how little we have been taught about facing death more honestly and directly. This most obvious reality of death is always in the background of our daily lives, sometimes coming more to the forefront but often just hovering in the dark shadows.

Do we need to have terrorists strike dramatically or experience natural disasters to remember the fragility of life? Do we need to be touched closely by the death of a friend or have our own close-call auto accident to remember the delicate balance between life and death? It's just so damn awkward for us to deal with this topic directly!

As I mentioned early in this book, this conspiracy of silence, the foundation of the inheritance taboo, is even supported through the use of superstitious thinking. This thinking makes it taboo to discuss your own condition, talk to your dying parent, or even talk to your siblings or other family members openly about the inevitability of death out of fear of making what you are talking about more likely to occur.

> **!** This conspiracy of silence is the single most potent outcome of our denial of death. It means that dying parents who can't face death themselves never hand their daughters the gold ring or pearl necklace they always wanted her to have. It means sons are never

given the golf clubs, gold dress watch, or special personal keepsake from their fathers. It means that children are unable to hear their parents say good-bye to them and to finish whatever emotional business they have to finish together.

Not only is this conspiracy of silence taking place through not speaking, it's also taking place in written legal documents, in which parents might refuse to identify specific personal items they want each child to have. "Let them figure it out for themselves," they think. Or, "I don't want to deal with making those kinds of decisions and risk upsetting myself and everyone else."

This conspiracy of silence is the backbone of the inheritance taboo. In refusing to face death while we still have time to take care of material and emotional business, we also refuse to deal with assigning our possessions to our children. That is the reason why the inheritance taboo is so deeply ingrained in our culture. Unless we are willing to face our own mortality, we can't overcome the conspiracy of silence.

CONFRONTING THE CONSPIRACY OF SILENCE

When a family is in crisis because of a sick or dying parent, assuming the parent is still coherent and able to rationally discuss his inheritance wishes, what tools can they use to facilitate more open and honest discussion? How can these tools help siblings preserve their relationships and even strengthen them?

These questions may be asked from the point of view of the parent who is having to face dying and also from the view of family facing the crisis. Before giving tools for improving communication, we need to be clear that no one should ever be forced to talk about something like dying if they choose not to.

RESPECTING THE RIGHT NOT TO
TALK ABOUT DEATH OR DYING

One of the reasons children, other family members, and friends are hesitant to discuss a parent's condition, bring up the topic of dying, or ask about inheritance plans is out of respect.

> **!** Certain people simply are unable or unwilling to discuss death and dying directly. They are perfectly able to establish a will or trust. But they can't face their own feelings enough to discuss dying when it comes down to it. Some are just too afraid to face it. Others are trying to be sensitive to their children and friends and don't want to make anyone feel uncomfortable. We must remember that the inheritance taboo has prevailed for so long because—besides all the wrong reasons—there are also some good ones that people have used not to deal with the whole situation. And one of those "good" ones is when you can tell—through any direct or indirect statements or behavior—that someone is simply too afraid to talk about his feelings. This fear becomes pretty clear when we notice what gets avoided.

Sometimes parents may refer to their dying more indirectly, through a sarcastic comment or in a joking manner. For example, my mother—who could discuss most aspects of her dying directly but did not draw up a separate list indicating how items should be distributed—had a lifelong dear friend, Lucy. They both had multiple physical problems and were in their 80s. They were in daily phone contact and would get together for dinner at least a couple of times during the week. Their standing joke together was, "If you die first, I'll kill you!" They both thought this was funny. A parent may feel more comfortable discussing dying with a friend who is her own age and facing it as well, rather than with her children. Or they may discuss only selective aspects of dying, such as sharing one's beliefs about what happens when we die or asking others about their beliefs.

Dying parents may show they know what is happening by tying up loose ends, such as moving money around to consolidate their accounts, paying off outstanding debts, or meeting with an accountant or attorney, intent on making it easier for their children to deal with their estate.

Or they may say things that make it clear they know they are dying, with references to never seeing certain places again, or thanking people for everything they have shared. They may begin making gifts of money or objects to family and friends without being asked. They may visit certain places, like an old hometown, that they haven't been back to for many years. For a sizable percentage, this is the closest they will be able to get to facing their own dying—at least in terms of communicating about it with loved ones.

! *If you want to know how your parent will deal with his own death, watch how he deals with the deaths of his friends or other family members.* If he finds it difficult or impossible to talk openly about others' deaths, most likely it will be at least as hard when it comes to his own.

In line with respecting your parent's right not to discuss dying, it's best to take your cue from him as to how open or direct to be in asking questions. While respect for limitations may be shown by not putting him on the spot by asking very direct questions, your concerns may be expressed in a different fashion.

Do not expect your parent or sibs to suddenly be able to pour their hearts out to you about their feelings about dying or inheritance if your family history is one of people being verbally guarded. You are sure to end up disappointed and frustrated if you do.

VALUING DEATH AND LETTING GO OF ATTACHMENT

Not only do parents literally hold on for dear life, but children, relatives, and friends do, too! *The most challenging task of dealing with your parent's condition will be to let him die rather than to fight to keep him alive.*

Not only will your parent have difficulty letting go of his attachment to his body, personality, and life, but you will, too. You will find yourself telling your dying parent to live *just a while longer* so that you may enjoy his company, guidance, and love. You will resist the process of death because you will be afraid that death is not only a bad thing for your parent, but a terrible thing for you, too.

Let your parent decide for himself when he is ready to go. He will be going through enough struggle letting go of his attachment to his body and personality. He will be fearful that merging into Oneness means giving up his individuality. Resist the strong temptation to try and cajole him into staying alive just because you can't bear to let him go. Give him "permission" to let go and give up the body.

It can be extremely painful physically and psychologically to let go of our attachment to this life. Those who are "late" in letting go of attachments will find it especially difficult to let go gracefully. *Perhaps the single most powerful act you can do for your parent is to face your own fear of death and not to let it influence your parent.* A world of difference exists between someone who is ready to die and can focus on letting go versus someone who is hanging on to each breath and is terribly fearful of dying.

Even what appear to be rather benign efforts to help your parent may send subtle messages to him that you can't let him die and that you don't value death. Or that you don't value your parent's right to choose when he wants to die.

For example, for about six months before my mother's death, I would tell her it was okay to go when she wanted to—not to hang on when she'd had enough. We never had a serious discussion about this, but she always listened when I said it. I began saying this more often after her first hospitalization, a couple of months before she died.

In the last few weeks of her life, she had trouble swallowing. In addition, she had lost her appetite and didn't want much to eat. While part of me interpreted this as her body beginning to shut down in anticipation of death, the part of me that was attached didn't want to pay attention to this message.

Instead, I would play the role of nurturing parent and feed her soup, one spoonful at a time. She would eat to please me and pretended she liked it, but I could see she really didn't want it. What appeared to be a loving gesture on my part was also a subtle attempt to keep her alive. I would frequently tell her to eat in the last few weeks of her life rather than let her stop eating, when that was what she wanted. Only upon later reflection did I fully comprehend my own message to her of valuing life over death—despite my repeatedly telling her to let go when she was ready.

But this moment of letting go of attachment to life and valuing death is further down the line. So let's take a step back and look at the tools that help us communicate with our parents and sibs before we get to this end point.

COMMUNICATION TOOLS

Keep in mind that how deeply you go will be determined by the long history in your family for communication to be relatively open or closed. It will also be determined by how deeply your parent wishes to connect with you and other family members.

- *Use "I" language and "soft" questions to express your feelings and concerns.* Rather than put the other on the spot, gently begin to share your own concerns. For example: "Mom, I'd really like to know the history of the family heirlooms. Could you tell me about those things that have meant so much to you? What is the history of this old silver wine cup?" Or: "Mom, I'm wondering if there are any wishes you have regarding your possessions. Is there anything specific you want any of us to have? Have you written down anywhere how you want your possessions to be divided?" Or: "Mom, I want to make sure I'm clear on your wishes regarding life support (or living conditions, life insurance, gifts, etc.). Do you feel up to talking about it?" This is an *invitation*—not a demand. Because there are so many practical issues that need to be addressed, there are plenty of chances to open this kind of dialogue.
- *Work with the various layers of resistance in the family by moving from one level to another, gently testing the next most indirect level before*

narrowing in on the most direct level. For example, if you see from your parent's behavior that he or she is unable to bring up anything having to do with inheritance directly, be respectful of this limitation but make an attempt to discuss relevant issues with your other parent, if there is one. Sometimes, this person is the gatekeeper of what is permissible to discuss. If your other parent can face the issues, open a dialogue with this person. This may pave the way to later talking with your dying parent more directly. If the surviving spouse seems unwilling or unable, then move on to your sibs and other family members such as aunts, uncles, or cousins.

Again, by using "I" statements that express your own concerns, you will quickly be able to assess who is able and willing to join you in dialogue and who isn't. The most difficult area of engagement will be discussing unfinished emotional business with your parent who is consumed by his physical condition. Even inheritance preferences will be easier than dealing with the old resentments accumulated over a lifetime. This is why it's far preferable not to wait to resolve these matters until a parent is suffering.

- *Consider using outside experts to help initiate family dialogue.* Psychologists, marriage counselors, trained personnel at senior facilities, or hospital support groups or other agencies may be able to help open the communication, which the family may then continue on its own. Especially trained to help in this regard are hospice workers, who may be brought into the family setting to help facilitate discussion. Simply facing the business issues by talking to one's accountant, attorney, or financial planner may also make talking about feelings easier. If your parent wants to talk but is unsure how much others can handle, the use of outside experts might be all that is needed to get the ball rolling.
- *Don't confuse your own need to finish emotional business with your parent's need.* Be clear when it is *your* need you are operating from, so that you may assess what nonverbal forms of expression may help sat-

isfy you if it becomes clear your parent is not interested in dealing with this.

- *Use indirect or nonverbal forms of emotional expression for communicating your feelings to your parent when verbal expression appears impossible or unproductive.* While it may be very necessary to discuss inheritance issues with your sibs and maybe other family members, it is *not absolutely necessary* that they be discussed with your dying parent, especially if he or she already has done some estate planning. When it comes to your own expression, remember that there are many indirect ways for you to share your love and begin the process of "saying good-bye" to you parent.

  For example, you can make a concerted effort to call your mother more often, spend more time with her, go out of your way to express your appreciation for what she has given you over your lifetime, and help pay for her care, if needed. You can take the time needed to make calls so that she receives whatever help she needs, and you can take on certain tasks yourself that express your love. You can write more frequent notes that share lifelong sentiments and/or send e-mail that keeps you in touch. You can sit down and write checks to pay bills for her. Or you can organize and clean her house when you visit, take her out to dinner, or bring in food for her, or in other big and small ways show her what she means to you.

- *Verbally express your love and affection.* If you are used to expressing affection verbally, do more than you are used to doing. If you are not used to this direct expression, experiment being more direct by making sure that every contact you have ends by saying, "I love you. You mean so much to me. Thank you for being in my life and caring for me." While you can't change your personality radically or the style of communication that has been learned and reinforced over a lifetime, you can allow yourself to risk saying loving things to your parent, *whether or not* your parent is able to reciprocate.

- *Express your feelings nonverbally through touch.* Rub your mother's feet. Help her take any medications she needs to take. Help dress her or feed her if she needs it. Give her a gentle back message or help her walk. Comb her hair. Do some of the things that were done for you when you were a child. Doing these kinds of things that feel like a role reversal, where you are nurturing your parent, can be a potent way to show your love. They are tangible and help neutralize any feelings of powerless over a disease. They may also make it easier for your parent to be able to verbalize her feelings.

- *Express your feelings by looking into your parent's eyes.* Making eye contact and holding it is the fastest way to get past your preoccupation with your parent's deteriorating physical body. It is the best way to connect to the "soul," or that essence that transcends identification with the body. In the everyday world, simply looking into someone's eyes will immediately connect you more deeply than any words that may be spoken. This is especially true if a parent is struggling with speech because of his or her condition.

- *Learn how to be a good listener.* Your parent may want to talk about all kinds of things unrelated to illness, dying, or inheritance. If you have many months of contact in your period of crisis, remember that being a good listener can be a powerful way to connect to your parent. To be a good listener, you must get your own needs out of the way, and let your parent's need to talk take center stage. In being a good listener, do not judge what your parent chooses to focus on; instead, understand that he has his own way of wanting to relate to each child.

   For example, during the last few months of my mother's life, when I would visit she would ask me to tell her about what good times I remembered while growing up. She wanted to go back to the pleasant family occasions and to reinforce the good feelings of how it had been when she was doing what she loved the most—being a mother to her children and sharing family outings. So I would tell her some of the family times that stood out for me that I knew she would remember. Then she would smile and tell me some of the times that she remembered. She wanted to meditate on these happy times and bathe in the good family life she had created and of which she had been the center.

- *Keep in mind that communication at any level will positively affect the whole family* and increase the chances of siblings being able to cooperate with each other over inheritance issues. The more united the children feel in caring for their parent, the better their chances of working out any problems when it comes time to dealing with the division of personal possessions. Although there are other factors that may interfere (such as past rivalries) once the parent dies, mutual cooperation while the parent is alive creates a positive and more loving example that may be carried forward during grieving and dealing with estate issues.

EXPLORING YOUR BELIEFS AND VALUES

For the following questions to be most valuable, take some time to think about your answer for each one of them. Write them down as you go through the list. This will not only make you consider each question more thoroughly, it will also assist you when you come back later and review your answers. Resist the temptation to disregard a question by jumping on to the next one before answering it. Also notice which of your answers to these questions make you uncomfortable. Come back to these questions whenever family experiences suggest the need to ask them more deeply. They may also be answered together with your sibs to initiate discussion.

1. What seems most important about our past for me to communicate to my parent about our relationship? Would I prefer to say it in person? Speak it in an audio- or videotape? Write it in a letter or e-mail? Or a combination?
2. What resentments do I have that are difficult for me to acknowledge to myself, whether or not I would ever say them to my parent?
3. Do I feel my parent has favored one of my siblings over me? How much does it bother me? How has my parent favored me?
4. Am I willing to consider bringing up any lifelong favoritism that my parent has shown one of my sibs?

5. If I'm willing to bring it up, what is it I want to hear from my parent that would help me feel more finished? Do I just want to hear that I matter, too? Or am I looking for an apology?

6. If I'm not willing to bring it up, what do I need to accept about my parent and the sib in question that would help me feel finished enough to let this go?

7. Am I willing to accept my parent's preference to give another sib money or possessions that I'm not given?

8. What are my beliefs about my need to be taken care of by my parent when he dies? Do I believe he owes me anything for what I have done for him? If so, exactly what is it I believe is owed?

9. What are my beliefs and values regarding what happens when I die? Are these beliefs in any way influencing my thinking when it comes to being open with my parent? Do they make it easier or more difficult to be open?

10. What am I willing to do during this crisis to get closer to my sibs, if I can? What am I willing to ask for from them in the way of emotional support? If I'm not willing to ask, do I believe they should just give it?

11. How much do I value my relationships with my sibs? More than my interest in fighting for certain possessions? Or does my inheritance seem more important than my relationships with my sibs?

12. What would I be willing to do to show my sibs that my relationships with them matter? What are the conditions in which I would *not* compromise, even if it means the possibility of blood wars with them?

13. How do I feel about letting my sibs know that there are certain possessions of our parent that I would especially like to have?

14. Would I be willing to ask my parent directly to give me a gift while he is alive, a special object that I really want to have? How would I ask for this gift? Am I willing to accept a refusal without feeling terrible?

15. What are my biases about my sibs, based on how I see each of them, that might affect how I view them during the inheritance process? In other words, what judgments have I *already* made about each of them that I need to be aware of as we enter this process?

16. What do I share with my sibs that we might use to make this an easier time for all of us? What projects, games, or activities might we use to help us feel closer as we face this crisis? What connects us?

17. Is it permissible for me to think about inheritance issues when my parent is sick and dying?

18. Does my family have a stated or implied superstition about talking about death, thinking this may make it happen?

19. How willing am I to go against any family superstition, if there is one?

20. Can I find a way to attend to the medical issues of my parent in a caring, sensitive manner, but also think about inheritance issues that are best dealt with while my parent can make her wishes known?

Answering all of the above questions thoughtfully will help you identify some of the issues that may need to be resolved in your family. Since the answers to these questions may bring up related emotions, let's now identify some of the key emotions you can expect to experience.

KEY EMOTIONS DURING CRISIS

A few basic emotions tend to predominate during the inheritance process. These key emotions and some of their associations are the following:

- *Anger and Disgust:* at having to deal with the illness or death of your parent; at having to deal with what are perceived to be greedy, needy, and irrational siblings; at the willingness of sibs to fight with each other over minor items of little value; at the mental strain of having to set limits and even make threats to sibs and others who are trying to take objects that are not intended for them; at watching sibs and others lie, steal, and connive against their own family members; at the thought of how the dead parent would have been distraught to know that his children couldn't handle it more peacefully; at watching life-long relationships with those who are your own flesh and blood deteriorate with the loss of the parent.

- *Envy:* toward siblings, the surviving parent, or any other extended family members who you perceive to have been given gifts or other favors by the dying parent; especially toward sibs if gifts of money or heirlooms are given to one and not to others; toward sibs when the parent chooses to spend more time with one than the others or in any other way makes it clear through word or deed that one sibling is being given something exclusively.
- *Resentment:* toward sibs or extended family members for what they say or do in relation to the dying parent that you believe is inappropriate or disrespectful; toward sibs for your not being included in crucial decision making. (Resentment from the past is such a key issue as it informs sibs reactions that we will look at it in more detail in the next chapter.)
- *Love, Compassion, and Sympathy:* toward the ill parent for having to suffer pain from their medical condition, for the depression or anxiety they may be suffering related to coming to terms with the end of life; toward your sibs as all try to deal with the practical affairs related to the parent's medical and practical needs; toward your parent's elder friends who, in facing the death, are forced to experience it as one step closer to their own; toward yourself and your sibs for being emotionally vulnerable during the process of grieving and beginning a new life without your parent.
- *Sadness and Loss:* at having to watch the deterioration of the body and mind of your parent; at having to face death yourself indirectly through watching your parent die; in dealing with the shock and loss when your parent dies; at having to see the worst sides of your sibs surface when it comes to dividing estate possessions and, because of the bitter conflicts, imagining a more distant relationship in the future.
- *Confusion and Fear:* at having to make many decisions in a crisis with little time to consider, sometimes based on limited information; at the welter of emotions related to knowing your parent doesn't have long to live; confusion related to the feelings of depersonalization or numbing that take place after the death of your parent; confusion at how to get through the hours, days, and weeks following death and

how to attend to decisions that need to be made while grieving your loss; fear that later surfaces as you allow in at a deeper level that there is no longer a "buffer generation" between you and your own eventual death.

- *Depersonalization:* feeling sensations of numbness in the extremities and a sense of being outside of yourself as you witness the events related to the death and the reactions of others (funeral arrangements, obituary, informing family and friends, content of the funeral ceremony, and all the business around the estate that follows, etc.). This experience of "spectatoring" or being outside the events that are taking place is called *depersonalization* and is a common coping mechanism when we are bombarded with an emotional shock that is more than we can bear. This is why some family members appear to be calm after a death and are able to deal with all the details before the reality sinks in and they begin their grief and mourning.

- *Guilt:* over what you think you should have done to prolong the life of your parent; over not spending enough time with him in the final days, weeks, or months; over not saying or doing certain things to show more directly how you felt; over not taking the risk to face death more directly by saying "good-bye" to your parent. Guilt may also be experienced by way of obsessing on specific conversations with the parent in an attempt to find special meaning in them. Obsessing on events and final contacts and conversations may begin soon after the death of the parent and last for months following it.

Try to identify these emotions as they come up by putting a label on them. For example: "Ah yes, feeling resentment again that Johnny is unable to refrain from his temper outbursts." Accept that emotions are a normal part of dealing with a crisis specifically and the inheritance drama in general.

In the next chapter, we move on to understanding your own reactions toward your siblings during a crisis and to explain why emotional reactions become so strong during the inheritance process.

CHAPTER 9
INSIGHT INTO YOUR
EMOTIONAL REACTIONS

The most important psychological dynamic played out in relation to family inheritance is this: Not only will each sibling tend to bring out in the others whatever is unresolved over the course of their lives, but what surfaces will be *magnified and exaggerated*.

It will be exaggerated because of the emotional stress of dealing with death. Especially in those families having no surviving parent or a passive surviving parent to monitor or attenuate the adult children's behavior, intensified feelings are common. Keep in mind that having money and possessions up for grabs will also heighten tensions and raise the stakes. It will be magnified because of the sensitivity of the others involved, of them being less tolerant of irritation and frustration than they otherwise might be under less stressful circumstances. These conditions combine to open up the wounds of childhood in a way that may lead to especially vicious and painful behavior.

Adults revert back to their childhood emotional states and react to each other from these earlier states, even as they are trying to remain rational and behave like adults. But the strength of unresolved resentments that have been simmering for decades may overwhelm their attempts to maintain self-control. For this reason, the history of inheritance is fraught with so many bitter disputes leading to blood wars between siblings.

These unresolved childhood issues will be displayed in how siblings deal with the parent's death, estate management tasks, and the division of personal possessions. These issues may also spill over into relationships with other relatives and friends, particularly if they get involved in the process.

> **!** Especially when large sums of money or real property are not at stake, the *typical arguments around possessions may always be interpreted as an attempt to resolve these earlier conflicts.*

Usually it's *not* the monetary value of the objects themselves that we dispute; instead, we're responding to old feelings from childhood and young adulthood that have been brought back to our conscious awareness. When these objects have family history and we closely associate them with the parent, the objects themselves will bring back early feelings that may contribute to this reversion to an earlier time.

As a benign example, when I look at certain ceramic pieces that my mother acquired early in the life of our family and kept in her kitchen, I would immediately associate them with happy family times together. Some of the objects I could connect to specific family gatherings around the dinner table, as well as to my mother nurturing her family through the preparation of meals. I spent thousands of hours over the years talking to my mother in her kitchen.

Some of these pieces are older than I am. I can remember seeing them as part of my daily home life since I was a young child. Just looking at a piece, like a colorful old ceramic rooster that sat in a niche above her kitchen sink, could bring back very early memories. Objects like this elicit a sense of stability and permanence. The rooster became associated with my experiences and relationships in that kitchen over a lifetime. Every time I would return to the house over the years, these pieces would always be sitting in the same place. I ended up choosing this rooster when it came time to distribute my mother's possessions. When I chose it, my brothers and I were able to remember the good times that we had in this kitchen over the decades. So this is an example of a positive connection that may bring sibs closer, rather than one that creates antagonism. These attachments are much more powerful when you have lived in the same house for many years while growing up and the objects in the house remain relatively constant.

One reason this dynamic between sibs of eliciting unresolved issues is so powerful is that, for many, the imposition of the past is only barely conscious or not conscious at all. This means that you may find yourself reacting strongly to small things that are said or done by a sibling and have no idea where the strength of your response is coming from. Once you've become aware of and accepted the power of this psychological dynamic to shape your reactions, you can understand yourself and your siblings' reactions in a new light.

> **!** *You are struck by the realization that almost everything happening with family members in dealing with grieving and estate issues is a repetition in some form of what has occurred earlier in the relationship.*

The basic question following from this awareness of the power of the past is this: "What remains unfinished with this person?"

> **!** *The key to preventing and resolving inheritance disputes is to understand how this past is being played out.*

With this insight, you can choose not to allow the past to predominate. You can do this by not "taking the bait" when provoked by a sibling. You can also choose to resolve whatever the issues are, if your siblings are willing. But without the awareness that this is even taking place, these old patterns will simply repeat with a strength that will baffle everyone involved.

FEAR OF ABANDONMENT VERSUS FEAR OF ENGULFMENT

One of the dynamics unfolding for adult children during a crisis, as a parent is near death or has died, is the polarity of the fear of parental abandonment versus fear of parental engulfment. Again, we are often unconscious or only semiconscious of this fear, which first arises in infancy and early childhood. The concept, from developmental psychology and infant attachment theory, is that—depending on the type of mothering you received—you will tend to develop either a basic fear of being abandoned by those you love or of being engulfed (or smothered) by them. There are degrees of severity on each end of the spectrum.

If our mother is overbearing, overprotective, and resists allowing us to separate adequately from her in the early years, she sets in motion the fear of engulfment. The mother resists letting us establish a separate sense of self, consequently promoting overdependence.

By not allowing us as infants and young children to freely explore our world, we become fearful of taking the necessary literal and psychological steps into the unknown. We are taught that everything is potentially dangerous and that we must stay close to our mother at all times. While we want this protection from our mother when we are very young, we learn to resent the feeling of fear, worry, and constriction that come with it as we get older.

As children, we fear taking risks without our mother's protection. We count on her to tell us what to do and how to do it and never learn to trust our own judgment. Our mother may tell us too quickly how to do something, what to believe about the world, and how to deal with other people. She focuses far too much on our helplessness and on her omnipotence and she doesn't understand our need to begin to assert our own independence and to make our own mistakes.

While Dad may say, "Stand up to that bully who pushed you," Mom tells us that he is dangerous and that we should be sure to stay away from him. She may prematurely call the school authorities and report the incident or—more drastically—even come to school and talk to the teacher to make sure we are safe. Mothers who create the fear of engulfment pattern can't tell when they are going too far to protect us.

They don't have a good sense of the boundary between mother and child and react to us as children as if we aren't really separate from them. They always err on the side of being too intrusive.

When we are not allowed to develop our own sense of identity separate from our mother, we become confused as to our own thoughts, beliefs, and emotions. We aren't sure whether we are really feeling what we think we are feeling or only feeling what we *should* be feeling.

It is common to hear the overbearing mother tell us as children what we are feeling. She will actually deny our own experience when we say we're feeling tired or hungry and tell us that we're not really tired at all. She will force us to finish everything on the plate whether we like it or not. And she short-circuits our attempt to have preferences by trying to define what is right for us.

Our mother may physically smother us with her body, forcing us to hug or kiss her more often and more intensely than we can stand. She may continue a pattern of being physically intrusive for many years without regard to the feedback we give her.

While engulfment may initially feel like love and caring to us as children, we learn as we get older how many choices and decisions we were not permitted to exercise. And we begin to resent our mother for creating our feeling smothered by her and then "act out" in opposition to assert our own independence and sense of self.

We fear not only being engulfed by our mother, but also by others with whom we try to be intimate as we mature. Both men and women may experience this pattern of overprotection and overdependence.

As adults, we display the fear of engulfment as the need to maintain adequate physical and emotional space from parents, spouse, siblings, and other relatives and friends. Sometimes, those of us who are more on this side of the polarity will favor a lot of time alone, and prefer intimate relationships in which we feel in control and are not pushed beyond our comfort limits of intimacy. We may also have trouble verbalizing feelings to family and friends, making demands, getting angry, or asserting ourselves with others.

The demand for either emotional expression or putting feelings into words may expose us to possibly being shamed and embarrassed, especially if we are not highly verbal and educated. Trusting that we will not be asked to give more in a relationship than we believe we have available becomes an issue.

Another manifestation may be problems with establishing a healthy sexual relationship that satisfies us and our partners. In addition, we express the fear of engulfment by needing to keep an emotional distance from our children and friends.

Others may view those fearful of engulfment as aloof, socially awkward, and unskilled at connecting well with work associates. Some dislike being a part of social activities in which demands may be placed on them to get along with people who want more than we have to give.

> **[!]** How does this fear of engulfment relate to death and inheritance? By adult children defending against being overwhelmed. We do this by keeping our emotional distance while the parent is sick and dying. And, after death, we defend against feelings of loss by limiting our involvement with siblings and other family members who may wish to offer various forms of support. Our mourning process may be less intense and of shorter duration than that of a child who fears parental abandonment.

Those adult children who defend against the fear of abandonment have experienced higher separation anxiety with their mothers in infancy and early childhood. While an engulfing mother errs by not allowing her child to separate from her, the abandoning mother errs by not knowing how to adequately attach and/or stay attached to her child.

Abandoning mothers are often young, immature, and plagued by their own insecurities and personal problems that interfere with their ability to form a close attachment and then stay connected to their infants. They may themselves have come from families in which the mothering they received was inadequate.

Our fear of abandonment may develop if the mother is absent or unpredictable or both in her caregiving habits; loves only conditionally, when we behave, but rejects us when we misbehave; is unable to provide a constant and stable presence in our life; is unaffectionate, poor at nurturing, or unable to protect or respond to us in times of need; or physically assaults, verbally abuses, or threatens to or actually does abandon us as a means of punishment.

If our relationship has been abruptly severed from either parent through death or other circumstances, such as divorce or a parent who abandons the home without returning, fear of abandonment will become our primary defense. As adult children with abandonment fears, we will demonstrate this concern in establishing love relationships and friendships. We will interpret the least negativity or criticism by a partner as a threat of abandonment. Any perceived loss or change in our lives makes us anxious. Our fear will sometimes lead us to become eager pleasers and accommodators to guard against the threat of others leaving us.

Or we may do the opposite: Rather than trying hard to hold on to the partner by any means, we instead keep ourselves emotionally distant so we will not feel the pain of separation and loss should a relationship not work out. Some of us will display a strong ambivalence that combines features of both—we will be clinging and needy for periods and then suddenly pull away and be emotionally distant and unapproachable. It may seem like we are two different people, one who wants too much and the other who doesn't want anything. We may have trouble finding a middle ground in relationships. The drama that often goes with our radical swings can be exhausting for those trying to relate to us.

> **!** During the crisis of dying and then the death of a parent, those of us who primarily fear abandonment will usually have a tougher time coping emotionally. We will use the defense mechanisms of denial and rationalization to ward off fears of abandonment during the dying phase. We may not view the illness as life-threatening, for example, and downplay the need to set limits on the parent when needed. We may hide behind wishful thinking that a medical cure may be found. When we are forced to come to grips with the parent dying, we may focus on our *own* fear of loss rather than on how difficult it must be for our parent to face death. We may also try to surround ourselves with other

people and parental possessions to help lessen the pain of feelings of abandonment.

After death, we can expect to experience the shock of loss of the parent more severely than the adult child who fears engulfment. In fact, those smothered adult children who have lived a lifetime with especially domineering and controlling mothers or fathers secretly may even feel some relief (along with guilt for feeling this relief) that the parent is no longer alive to control them.

But as a child who fears abandonment, we must deal with our worst nightmare. We're forced to be on our own in what appears to be a cold and lonely world. We are unsure of our ability to survive without our parent to protect us. Our best refuge is to have a spouse or friend who tries to play a substitute role to attenuate our feelings of abandonment.

As a child who fears abandonment, we may experience a stronger desire to preserve the personal possessions of the parent, to take over the parent's home, if there is one, or to surround ourselves with as much of the "vibration" of the parent as possible, such as wearing his or her clothing, jewelry, etc. Because we psychologically experience (and focus on) the parent as personally abandoning us rather than simply dying, we may also go through a more complicated bereavement process, including anger and rage at the "final abandonment" of death.

> **[!]** Why is this dynamic of abandonment versus engulfment important? Because if you can decipher which side of the equation you identify with, you will have some insight as to your predicable reaction upon the death of your parent. You may also be more able to understand the reaction of your siblings.

Children from the same mother don't necessarily have the same experience with the mother. This will have more to do with the particular unique early attachment experienced with the parent, as well as the relationship maintained with the parent into adulthood. It will also have to do with individual experiences each child has with intimacy and loss with others as he matures. But it's true that when the mother is *especially* engulfing or abandoning, the chances are higher that all siblings will have the same predominant fear.

Our fears of abandonment versus engulfment may not necessarily be conscious or very powerful. But it is a good place to start your inquiry: Ask yourself, based on the type of mothering you received, which side of the polarity you most closely identify with, and consider how your identification may affect your reactions to grieving and in dealing with your sibs during the inheritance process.

The following behaviors are more likely to typify those who fear abandonment by the parent:

√ Lives close to the parent throughout their life; never moves very far away

√ Frequent and lengthy (three or more times per week) phone contacts and/or visits (not including health crisis conditions) is the typical pattern of contact

√ Reacts strongly to the least perceived slights by parent

√ Avoids confrontations if at all possible, prefers to go along passively with parental preferences

√ Exhibits frequent and obvious "sucking up" behavior to gain parental favor and approval, and makes efforts to gain favor of parent over sibs

√ Enjoys taking vacations with parents and spending all major holidays with them

√ May exploit parent/grandchild relationship to solidify parent/child bond

Asks for financial help from parent but often keeps debt running for years, both out of sense of entitlement and to increase enmeshment with parent

For those who are more fearful of engulfment, typical behaviors include the following:

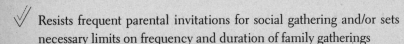 Resists frequent parental invitations for social gathering and/or sets necessary limits on frequency and duration of family gatherings

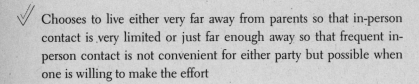 Chooses to live either very far away from parents so that in-person contact is very limited or just far enough away so that frequent in-person contact is not convenient for either party but possible when one is willing to make the effort

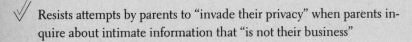 Resists attempts by parents to "invade their privacy" when parents inquire about intimate information that "is not their business"

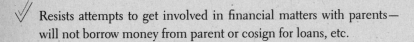 Resists attempts to get involved in financial matters with parents— will not borrow money from parent or cosign for loans, etc.

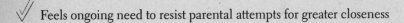 Feels ongoing need to resist parental attempts for greater closeness

UNRESOLVED ISSUES SURFACING DURING CRISIS

In addition to the type of early mothering resulting in either fear of abandonment or engulfment, here are some of the more common unresolved psychological/emotional issues we have that may resurface during crisis.

Inclusion/Exclusion
Have you felt basically included in your family during your early years and into adulthood? Or have you felt excluded by parents or siblings? How about with extended family members, such as aunts, uncles, and

cousins? Have you had much relationship with nieces and nephews? Have there been any dramatic ruptures in relationships with parents causing long separations in contact? How strongly have you felt about family members being close to you? How much have you avoided or limited contact or involvement with your family?

If you have felt excluded by parents, sibs, or extended family over many years, you may be overly sensitive to issues of fairness and equality in the disposition of possessions. You may also emphasize fairness even if you've felt included but saw a pattern of siblings being favored over you for time, attention, and gifts. Because feelings of inclusion/exclusion are not common topics for family discussion, these individual judgments family members made may never be tested by comparing them with the perceptions of others.

Does it matter how others see you if you feel left out? It matters because you may not be left out so much as not feeling as intimate and included as you would like.

One of the reasons some adult children ask their dying parent for certain symbolic or meaningful possessions is to feel closer to the parent. When we receive the object we hope it makes up for our deeper feelings of a lack of love and approval. It also helps us prepare for the loss of the parent.

For example, Robert now lives on the West Coast while the rest of his family live in the Midwest, where they have been settled all their lives. After college graduation, Robert was the only one of his sibs to move away from his hometown. While his sibs are in close contact with one another and with their parents, Robert feels excluded from intimate family contact. He experiences this in two ways: When he visits, he doesn't think his family gives him the attention that they ought to, and he is kept out of the loop when there is family news. He sees there is a price to pay for daring to fly away from the nest.

Approval/Disapproval by Parents

Have you felt basically loved and accepted by your parents? Have your choices for career path, marriage partner, lifestyle, and how you've conducted yourself as an adult resulted in parental approval or disapproval?

Has the approval received been *conditional*—given only when you measured up to a certain standard? Or has it been constant and unconditional over your life, so that you knew you were loved and accepted even when you didn't measure up? This issue is further complicated by the fact that even when there is "good enough" mothering and you feel approved of, we always wish for *more*. If your parents haven't unconditionally loved and accepted you, this issue is sure to rear its head during crisis and after death.

Over the close to thirty years I have practiced psychotherapy, perhaps the single common denominator among those I've worked with is their feeling that their parents loved them only conditionally. This sense of conditional love is so pervasive that a specific example isn't even necessary. It's safe to say that there isn't a single person reading this who doesn't know from his or her personal experience what it means to be loved conditionally, at least at some period of their life.

As I go to great lengths to show in my book *When Good Enough Is Never Enough*, striving for parental love and approval is built into our culture. It contributes to perfectionism and various other kinds of problems.

Approval/Disapproval by Sibs

To what degree do you feel your sibs have respected your choices in life and the path you have chosen for your career? How do you think they feel about the way you've conducted yourself in business matters with them? Or in showing them that you care for them as brothers or sisters?

What tangible evidence have you to support your belief that they approve or disapprove of you? How do you think they regard your morals and ethics? How do you imagine they would describe you to others who know you? How much does it matter to you whether or not they approve of you? What efforts have you made to impress them with your accomplishments or to elicit comments of approval?

Resentments

A resentment is a bitter anger or ill will relating to the past. The power of the original hurt and anger may diminish over time, only to be reignited when someone says or does something that brings up the old feelings. Since most families are not good at resolving interpersonal conflicts to the satisfaction of all concerned *as they arise*, it's easy for resentments about disagreements or slights to build up over the lifetime of the family relationship. They may be covered over for years before resurfacing during crisis.

> ⚠ *Resentments are powerful when the emotion behind them is powerful.* This is why we don't forget them, no matter how much time may pass.

> ⚠ *Resentments are the first place to look when you want to understand your actions during the inheritance process.*

Earlier, when we asked ourselves the question "What is unfinished with this person?" we were looking for possible sources of resentment. Everything that sibs may argue and disagree over may be fuel for resentment held over many years.

Resentments will relate to the other unresolved issues we are identifying here. For example, you may resent your brother never showing the interest in you or your family that you believe he should have shown. Or you may resent your sister for never making the same effort you've made to care for others in your family. Resentments are always from past hurts. But we experience them more as seething anger than as conscious hurt. They are not the same as envy for things your sibs have that you don't or for jealousies, like believing your father likes your sister more than he likes you.

Other common resentments include money lent or given to a sib or his children by a parent; favors shown a sib or his children; instances of feeling rejection, disrespect, or humiliation that may go back to childhood; promises made but never kept; disappointed expectations about the level of closeness that was hoped for; irresponsible behavior such as not honoring commitments made; and various other perceived or real slights that were never resolved when they occurred.

Mary's uncle, for example, never forgave her for speaking up at a family gathering when she heard him berating her mother, who was cooking holiday dinner for the family. Her crime was to tell her uncle to stop speaking to her mother in such a harsh fashion. Her uncle, who was neurotic, touchy, and too quick to take offense, couldn't handle her comments. He left the house in a huff, sped out the driveway, and never again spoke to Mary. He banished her from his life for over a decade. Mary, thinking she hadn't done anything wrong, never believed it was her obligation to apologize for her behavior. This is an example of a long-term resentment resulting from one family member speaking up for another. It hurt Mary's mother that her brother could not forgive her daughter, and she also felt badly that she had been the cause for the words that created the break between two people she loved.

Nurturance/Distance

Both for parents and sibs, the amount of nurturing we've received versus how far the other has distanced herself from us. This is not the same as inclusion/exclusion, in that you may feel included in your family but not feel that you are as close to your parents or sibs as you would like to be. A significant degree of the resentment created over the life of a sibling or parental relationship is due to disappointment we feel when our need for nurturance isn't met. However, for the child afraid of engulfment, the theme of creating sufficient distance will dominate that of not being adequately nurtured.

Part of growing into adulthood means we have to face the reality of unmet expectations of a higher degree of closeness and nurturance from family members than we actually receive. "Good" mothering means adequate (but not overpowering) nurturance, while inadequate mothering means creating too much distance so that children never feel the protective security that allows them to go out into the world and stand on their own emotional feet.

One of the interesting dynamics related to this issue is how, in some families, a sib will ease into the role of nurturer when a parent dies. It may be the oldest or the one who is most identified as the caregiver. But in families that include nurturing females, it appears to be quite common. In families where there are no females, a spouse may play this part for her partner. She may actually take on some of the characteristics of her husband's mother in an attempt to help fill the void.

Dependence/Independence

Related to the above, this is a function of how safe a child is made to feel so he may go out on his own, both in conquering developmental stages when young (going to school, learning to function without parental support, taking on the added responsibility of holding a job, etc.) as well as in managing the adult challenges that follow.

Did your parents promote independence in behavior and thinking? Or did a strict compliance to rigid standards and beliefs constrict your behavior? Adult children who have been heavily dependent on a parent will have a more difficult time dealing with loss. They will feel unprepared to take care of themselves, which will influence their expectations of their siblings, especially when it comes to feelings of entitlement. In other words, they will expect sibs to take over where the parent left off by giving them special treatment.

Sibling Rivalry for Achievement

The basic competition between sibs is initially played out to win love, approval, and favor from parents and, later, significant others, such as teachers and employers. This rivalry takes a number of forms, both direct and indirect. It may result in a high degree of arguing, comparing, backbiting, and one-upmanship between sibs, as they vie for what is perceived to be the limited amount of love and approval available from parents.

Sibling rivalries continue into adulthood—not only because they are reinforced by the larger society in the form of competition in the workplace, sports, and in the achievements of their own children, but also because sibs never quite give up the notion that parents will give more love and approval when they are proud of the child's achievements.

Children learn that the parent's approval will be *conditioned* upon achieving at a high level in relation to others, including their own brothers and sisters. The comparison between sibs is not only for the parent's favor but also as a way of gauging their own accomplishment. They may measure this by job status, income, professional or community recognition; accomplishments of their respective children; or status as measured by houses, cars, type of vacations, and other status symbols, such as the cost of various personal possessions.

Contact with/Withdrawal from Siblings

By this I mean the tendency to stay in relatively ongoing contact with parents and sibs versus withdrawing from contact. It also includes the *quality and directness* of contact. For example, some may be in online contact by way of e-mail and instant messaging and by phone, while others will make the added effort to visit in person. A healthy rhythm of contact and withdrawal is necessary in all human relationships. Too much contact results in feeling smothered, while too much withdrawal results in feelings of distance or disconnection.

Sibs will establish and reestablish their patterns of contact and withdrawal over a lifetime. Although the degree and frequency of contact vary, it's easy to settle into patterns that tend to become relatively stable. The source of many resentments can be the difference in their desires for the amount and quality of contact with each other.

Locus of Control/Power

This is how much you believe you can control event outcomes (internal locus of control) versus how much you believe they are in others' control (external). To the degree that you view others as determining what happens to you rather than you being responsible for what happens affects how much you view your sibs as doing something to deprive you of inheritance money or possessions.

When we feel power over another person, we believe we have control over that person's outcomes. Those who focus the locus of control externally tend to be blamers. Those who perceive the locus of control as internal tend to be more active at trying to influence events and others to their preferred outcomes. They may err in believing they may affect events more than they actually can. But at least they make the effort to shape what happens rather than sit back and passively allow things to happen to them.

This issue is relevant because parents who overcontrol their children are more likely to produce adult children who experience the locus of control externally rather than internally. These children become vigilant at detecting cues from others, especially authority figures, as to desired behavior and work toward using those cues to shape their behavior for approval.

Peggy, for example, could not stop blaming others for all the terrible things that happened to her. If she didn't get the work project she wanted, she blamed her colleagues. If she had a disagreement with her mother, it was always something her mother had done, not her. Her theme was to blame the world for everything that didn't work out.

She even blamed me for not agreeing with her perception of the world and for telling her that disowning her own part in what she created was a distortion of reality and only made her feel powerless. It took her three years of work with me for her to begin to assume responsibility for her own actions and outcomes. And she fought me almost every bit of the way. But as her whining about the world began to subside, she took new risks and discovered that her blaming everyone for so long was based on modeling she received from her inadequate mother. Ultimately, she learned to transcend blaming even her mother.

INHERITANCE ROLES AND UNRESOLVED ISSUES

Now that we've identified the common unresolved issues among family members, we need to connect these issues to some of the main roles that family members play, which we identified earlier in Chapter 3. I want to show you how specific roles played by "receivers" (or beneficiaries) relate to these issues. This will make it easier for you to assess which dynamics may be playing themselves out once you have identified your role. The following are examples.

The Wicked One: Filled with resentment and bitterness and intent upon lashing out vindictively in any way possible. If a sibling, often exhibits strong rivalry in which she feels like she has not measured up; feels excluded from family, received insufficient approval from parents and sibs. Often feels cheated, victimized, or taken advantage of in some way, and views the inheritance process as a chance to "get even." These issues may also fit for *The Second Wife/Husband*, *The Adopted Child*, and *The Problem Child*. Common to all of them are feelings of resentment and bitterness.

The Favorite Child: Moderate to strong feelings of sibling rivalry despite being favored by parent; feels included and approved of, but may be overly dependent on parent emotionally and materially; may also create dependency feelings on part of parent, especially when needing more personal care during illness and dying; feelings of being favored help defend against emptiness and loss; strong feelings of entitlement, which come through both in expectations related to inheritance and in expecting sibs to continue special treatment when parent dies; does not understand when sibs refuse to play the same role as did the parent in excuse making, bailing out of trouble, gift giving, etc. Some of these expectations will also exist with *The Trust Fund Child* and *The Daddy-Doll Girlfriend*.

The Child Who Has His Own: Often feels included and approved of, with the exception of those who have split off from family and have little contact because of early bad blood; often feels nurtured by family but may create physical or emotional distance in needing less from family materially and emotionally; prides himself on taking care of himself financially and is therefore less likely to get caught in becoming financially entangled with and dependent upon the parents. Because of this, may feel resentment that sibs and other family members are given more money, gifts, and loans as a matter of "fairness." While the parent believes it's fair (since the other sibs are more in need of financial help), this is more an issue of *equality* between sibs.

Those identified with this role have the advantage of being able to play a compromising part to help avoid sibling wars, as the money or possessions up for grabs may not be viewed as life-changing as it is for other sibs who feel more needy of the inheritance. As a result, this child is in good position to help settle disputes that may arise between other sibs.

The Second Wife/Husband: Feels on the periphery compared to children of her second husband; may feel resentment if time and attention have been competed for with her spouse's children for many years; children may also view her as competing for what they believe is rightfully theirs, especially when financial resources are such that there is "not enough to go around." *The Lost and Forgotten Child* and *The Adopted Child* may also feel left out compared to biological children who had greater intimacy with the parent.

HOW PARENTS CAN MINIMIZE SIBLING CONFLICT

I've identified various psychological dynamics that may be unconsciously reverted to during an inheritance crisis. Because they may be unconscious in no way means they aren't powerful enough to dictate your behavior. You simply won't know why you're reacting in the way you are. In addition, in the previous section, I have paired off some of the main sibling roles and their likely unresolved conflicts. By being aware of which role you are playing (both as you and your sibs perceive it), you'll be able to notice when you have strong reactions related to these early issues. Connecting your reactions to the past—rather than seeing your sibs as their cause—can itself go a long way in helping you temper your reactions.

Psychological motivators are also relevant in the decisions of parents. Here is a list of some of the things the trustor (giving) parent needs to consider during crisis but *before* he or she is preoccupied by illness and other distractions to help prevent family blood wars:

1. *Understand that you may be reacting to psychological needs and resistances when you choose to avoid dealing with inheritance disposition choices.* When you choose not to specifically spell out which child you wish to have certain possessions, you are making a statement about not caring enough who ends up with which items. If you feel this way, fine. But while you save yourself from having to make tough choices, you are increasing the likelihood that your children will argue about who gets what. It will *almost never* go as peacefully and lovingly as you would hope.

2. *Understand that by choosing not to designate who gets what items you may be unconsciously trying to guarantee that your children will not forget you* — but that their not forgetting your death (or your life) may be connected to conflict resulting from not having your wishes clearly spelled out. In other words, *to keep things unclear is a way to be remembered,* as the strong negative emotions your children will experience means a stronger association to you. Is that how you want them to associate these objects?

3. *Understand that just because you tell a child privately that you want her to have a specific possession when you die, this does not mean other children will believe this assertion, nor does it mean he or she will necessarily receive that item.* If it matters to you, give the child the possession before you die and let yourself enjoy her reaction to your gesture.

4. *Understand that it is not enough to simply say in your will: "Divide my possessions equally among my children."* As will be shown in the next chapter on dividing possessions, without a well-reasoned and systematically executed plan for the division of personal possessions, arguments and disagreements are more likely to occur.

5. *Understand that petty jealousies, envy, lifelong resentments, and sibling rivalries will mean that anything not put in writing or said in front of all siblings involved stands a chance of being disputed.* Even if you state your intentions in front of all children, the seriousness of your claims may be argued or a child may say you were not thinking clearly when you made your designation. You will no longer be alive to clear up their squabbling.

6. *Understand that your children will be grieving your death in the weeks
    and months that follow it. This will add to their confusion when trying
    to make decisions about dealing with your estate.*

7. *Understand that, while you are reasonably healthy and of sound
    mind, you can make it easier for your children during this grieving time
    by having your financial affairs in order and by taking the time to state
    clearly as part of your will or trust anything in particular you want to
    go to any of them.*

8. *Understand that giving your children anything you want them to
    have while you are still alive will be especially remembered and ap-
    preciated because you personally handed it to them.* In addition,
    you ensure there will be no dispute among sibs when you do it in
    this way.

9. *Understand that by personally giving your possessions to your children
    while you are alive, you are able to see their reactions, enjoy knowing
    they received the gift directly from you, and watch how much they may
    value the item while you are still alive.*

10. *Understand that by giving your prized possessions away yourself
    means you may also be able to use the occasion to discuss anything
    else, such as your hopes for them honoring certain beliefs or values of
    yours that you wish to pass down as part of your legacy.*

11. *Understand that forcing yourself to give away some of your prized pos-
    sessions to your children directly shows them you're able to face your
    death and may thus make it easier for them to deal with it, too.*

12. *Understand that the process of saying "good-bye" to your children
    will take some time for you and them to deal with all the possible is-
    sues that need to be discussed.* Therefore, begin it sooner rather than
    later.

As you are able to face your own death more directly, you will be giving "permission" for your children to face it more directly as well. They
will be looking to you for verbal and nonverbal cues to tell them how
open they can be with you. Greater openness will allow them to help
you and each other through the crisis, no matter how long or short it

may be. The more directly sibs can talk about their feelings, the closer they may feel in trying to negotiate this difficult period. This communication breaks down the inheritance taboo. It creates the emotional setting for openness, appreciation of different styles of grieving, and support to get through the pain.

Many of the above-listed points relate to being a good parent at the end of your life. You are coming full circle and doing some of the same kinds of things you did as a parent when your kids were young. You are teaching them lessons that you want them to remember, helping them solve disputes, and showing them your strength as you face the end of your life—just as you showed them when they were young.

This is a final chance for you to show your children how to conduct themselves. It is also a chance for you to express your love to them both directly and symbolically, just as you always have. Take advantage of the opportunity.

CHAPTER 10
POSSESSIONS LIVE FOREVER

When you consider it from the point of view of the relationships at risk, it's remarkable that the interest in inheriting possessions from a parent can mean so much. The history of families through generations shows us again and again the price some will pay just to have material objects, often ones that are of mostly sentimental and limited monetary value.

> **!** The price we are willing to pay is this: *We will make the objects more important than our relationship to our blood relatives*—those to whom we have often felt the closest and with whom we have shared some of the most significant events of our lives. We may not *admit* that we will risk it, but for those who won't compromise and whose resentments from the past take over to dictate their behavior, this is exactly what is at stake.

Even when we don't covet the object itself, our fear of losing out on something or having our sibs take advantage of us may take over. This impulse may lead to getting caught up in arguments over objects simply as a defensive maneuver to avoid being taken advantage of. This is why understanding how we are playing out past patterns is so important. If we aren't aware that we are reacting from issues from the past, we will find ourselves feeling righteous indignation. We may take a stand that threatens relationships over our parent's personal property that we don't really even want. But we can't stand the thought that our sibs may be getting something we aren't—just as we couldn't when we were children.

> [!] *If you take away only one key insight from reading this book, it*
> *should be how powerfully your emotional past with your sibs*
> *colors the inheritance process—especially the division of money and*
> *personal property.*

We will risk the future coherence of our family because we believe we must have some object that connects and bonds us to another member of our family. The object and the connection become more important than the real live relationship we have with a brother, sister, uncle, or aunt. Greed and pettiness may rule over honesty and a sense of integrity.

We will go so far as to steal or hide objects that we want. We will lie to our sibs about whether we have taken anything. And we will justify our actions to ourselves any way we can so that we don't feel guilty. We may even invoke the dead parent, believing "Mom wanted me to have this" to justify lying, stealing, or deceiving our sibs and other relatives. We may end up at odds with one of our parents over something the other parent promised to leave us but ended up in the hands of the second parent.

Given the power of personal possessions to create blood wars, it's important to understand *why* we are willing to risk relationships over personal property. While it's definitely true that objects of a parent who dies help keep us connected, it's only this way because of the meaning *we* imbue to the object and the association *we* make between the object and the parent.

This is made very clear when you see how differently siblings will value a particular item. While some items may be of equal interest to all, many have a particular meaning and value associated to them that will vary from child to child. While this may seem obvious, the reality of how it operates during the division of property is sometimes striking.

For example, I found there were many items of my mother's that my two brothers found to be of interest and value, while I had no interest at all. The fact that it was my mother's did not necessarily mean that I was interested in owning it. But as to those items I *was* interested in, I attributed value to them mostly because of the associations they held for me or the experiences I had with them.

Because we may be connected to the parent through photographs, letters, e-mail, and our complete memory bank of experiences with him or her, there is no one specific object *alone* that is going to connect us forevermore.

No matter how many of the parent's possessions we have, we may experience an unconscious fear of forgetting him, of losing the mental image that we ought to be able to recall at any moment. Despite having photographs, as time passes, some of us are afraid we will lose our sense of the "essence" of the parent. So we may want a bottle of perfume, clothes that have the distinctive scent of our mother, and anything else that we can use to reinforce our memory so that we don't forget the literal sense of the person.

I know this fear of forgetting the parent is true because I've heard it expressed by patients over the years in my clinical practice. Sometimes it is only a matter of months after the loss, and they are already fearful of forgetting the mannerisms and impact of the loved one. Children and adolescents express this fear very directly, as their storehouse of memories and ability to call on them is more limited. For adults, the stronger the attachment to the parent, the less likely they are to worry about losing the image.

We need to remember that as we negotiate with our siblings during the process of dividing personal property, *the objects themselves are not what really matters*. We can decide how little or how much we need to keep us connected to a parent. And this means that we can always compromise with a sibling for the sake of the future of our relationship— without feeling that we gave up something vital to our life just because we may not end up with what we want.

Again, no matter how valuable we may deem it, possessing any particular item is not necessary to the survival of our images and memories of the parent. So we can use the process of dividing personal property as an opportunity to give to our sib what she cares about more than we do. We may do this in service of going past our own desires for the sake of feeling a closer bond.

One of the problems that creeps in when there are lifelong sibling rivalries is that it is tough to switch gears and stop competing for the parent's possessions. With highly competitive siblings, it's easy to make the division of possessions a contest, each vying to get the "best" objects and not wanting to see a sib end up with something that they want. Instead of thinking longer term, it's easy for them to lapse into the mentality of "getting my share," of not being generous or even thoughtful of the other when it comes to letting a sib have something that may be more meaningful to her than it is to them.

But when we are aware of our tendency to get caught in the competitive aspect of the division of property, we may consciously decide to make decisions that result in closeness rather than in distance. Or, at least, decisions that don't push us any further away.

THE NEED FOR NURTURING AND THE HUNGER FOR POSSESSIONS

Why do we find it easy to get greedy, hungering for the parent's possessions? Sibling rivalries aren't the only ones that create the competitive setting. What we need to understand is that the death of a parent reawakens our early needs to be cared for, protected, and nourished by the parent. These needs are operating whether or not we are aware of them.

The adult child is confronted with the questions, "Who will protect me from the world, now that you are gone?" and "How will I fill the loss and emptiness that I feel?"

In facing and resolving these questions, we fully learn to stand on our own emotional feet, no longer needing to be soothed by our parents. This is why some developmental psychologists have maintained that we don't fully mature emotionally until our parents have died.

Because we have this fear of making our own way in the world without the nourishment and support from our parents, we may substitute inheritance money and property to fill the emotional loss and emptiness. If we can use this insight to understand the role possessions play during inheritance, we can consciously decide that we will fill that void in another way. By doing that, we are less likely to grasp for the parent's possessions.

As I mentioned earlier, for those who can adopt a long-term mentality, a parent's death is the perfect opportunity to make up for past perceived inequities between siblings and to set the foundation for a connected future. At least to some degree, our siblings, spouse, children, extended family, and friends may fill the emptiness that we are feeling in our loss of the parent. Similarly, we may find fulfillment in our work, hobbies, children, and other interests that sustain us in life.

Since our common loss is what connects us most deeply to our sibs in dealing with the inheritance situation, we can make the process of grieving more manageable when we consciously use the situation to support each other emotionally. But this is only possible when we focus more on the relationship to the person than on the relationship to the possessions up for grabs.

In support of the above, in some families one of the sibs—often the eldest but not always—will step forward and begin to assume some of the nurturing behaviors the parent who has died once performed.

For example, the eldest daughter will begin to look after her sibs more closely than she had before the death. She may consciously or unconsciously take over some of the mannerisms, habits, and nurturing behaviors of her mother. Or the most nurturing brother will begin to call his sibs more often to see how they are doing in handling their grieving. Likewise, he may begin to take on some of the habits of his father.

The obvious but penetrating realization by the sibs that "all we have now is each other" may elicit a spirit of togetherness and cooperation that transcends the typical petty bickering that often accompanies the division of the estate. It may draw sibs closer to the remaining parent, if there is one. And it may heighten our awareness that we don't have forever to spend time with our sibs and other family members, and so we ought to take advantage of what time we do have, actively including them in our lives.

Sometimes this awareness will lead to an interest in forging or renewing relationships with extended family, such as distant aunts, uncles, and cousins. This interest may lead to a sustained effort to stay connected. More often than not, however, when everyone goes back home to the faraway cities in which they live, it is easy for the connection efforts to be limited or to fall away. But even if this occurs, the whole family may still help each other through the funeral and their feelings of loss.

FORTY YEARS ON A HANDFUL OF POSSESSIONS

It makes good psychological sense to focus on *less* rather than *more* when it comes to inheriting personal possessions. Although the natural inclination is to always want more, I have learned that a handful of objects from a parent is enough to take you through a lifetime. Let me explain what I mean, using my own experience as an example.

As I mentioned in the preface, when I was 14, I watched in horror as my father died suddenly while lying on a sofa twenty feet in front of me. He was stricken by his fourth heart attack. I was just about to enter my last semester of junior high school. I was completely overwhelmed and dealt with the shock of his death by numbing myself to the world around me. To make matters worse, two months later John F. Kennedy was assassinated and the whole country experienced something of what I was already going through.

My mother did not give me a lot of my father's personal possessions, nor did I ask for much. I just wasn't thinking about wanting anything at the time. Rather than remembering anything, all I wanted was to *forget*. But my mother, who knew it would be good for me to have some of his things to help remember him by, offered me a few of them.

Perhaps not so surprisingly, what has been most meaningful to me in staying connected to the memory of my father over the last forty years are the things that I already had in my possession before he died. Very simple things, like a "snow dog" Saint Bernard statue with a barrel of liquor round his neck that sits on a platform with the name "Hennessy" inscribed prominently. Used for marketing the product, the statue was something my father picked up in a liquor store when I was a kid. He brought it home and handed it to me. I have it placed on a bookshelf that lines my office. I glance at it at least briefly every day when I walk in.

One of my prized possessions is a dirt-smudged baseball on a plastic stand that also sits on my bookshelf. My father caught it during a night game we went to see when I was about 10. For some reason, my brothers didn't go—it was only the two of us. We were sitting off the third-base line, in box seats with a great field view. When a sharply hit foul ball was lined our way by Dodger first baseman Norm Larker, my father leaned over the seats, managing to catch it in his bare hands. Although he bloodied his knee in the effort, he smiled and immediately handed the ball to me once he recovered from his effort.

His giving me the ball was perhaps the single most dramatic and loving gesture toward me that I can remember. What a magical night that was, as the Dodgers managed to come from behind and win the game. You could go to hundreds of games and never come close to catching a foul ball. And yet, on that night, the stars lined up for it to happen. Although I had always loved him deeply, my father became a real hero to me that night. The fact that he immediately and unselfishly handed me the baseball proved to me beyond the shadow of a doubt how much he loved me.

I also have the watch my father was wearing when he died. And I have a couple of the pipe tobacco humidors he used. I also have a few Dunhill pipes that were his. They are classics—the best made—and worth something to pipe smokers who appreciate the most prestigious name in pipes. I smoked them for years, until I was in my 30s.

And perhaps even more valuable to me—even if less dramatic in how it was obtained—is another baseball autographed by all of the Los Angeles Dodgers in 1959, the year they happened to win the World Series. I wanted a baseball signed by Duke Snider, who, for some reason that is not altogether clear to me now, became my slugging hero at the time. My father ended up having to write to the general manager of the team, as we had sent a few dollars to cover the cost of the ball but didn't receive one from Duke Snider.

I have the letter that my father sent to the Dodgers' general manager. I also have the reply from Buzzie Bavasi informing my father that they would be sending me a ball signed by the whole team with their compliments.

Why am I sharing this personal history? To show how it's this kind of stuff that has sustained me for over forty years since my father's death. I learned to value just a handful of items—none of any great monetary value—to help me remember what he meant to me over the short fourteen years I knew him. Although the World Series ball has some value in the memorabilia market, I wouldn't consider selling it, as it has far greater value in the "memory market" of my mind! Of course, I also have some family movies that I watch periodically, as well as the option to visit anytime I wish my mother's home (now my brother's), where we grew up.

> **!** Moral of the story: Don't get caught in thinking you need a lot of possessions to remember your parent or other family members when they die. The few things you have may translate toward a deeper and more profound meaning *the longer you live with them*.

PRESERVING FAMILY HISTORY AND RITUAL

Transferring personal possessions during inheritance carries on the history of the family. We maintain a sense of continuity and coherence as one generation passes down to another this history.

For example, a pair of fancy etched silver candlesticks that came from Russia had been passed down from my great-grandmother to my grandmother to my mother and then down to us. These candlesticks were valuable in and of themselves and were also symbolic of a family's migration from Russia to the "new world" of the United States. My mother used them for holiday celebrations. They were, perhaps, in terms of their history, *the* most important family heirloom.

The candlesticks not only served as an object of value that connected the heritage of the family, they also became part of the ritualistic celebration of holidays. Even without knowing their exact history, the whole family knew they had been a part of our legacy from our earliest memories. They are the kind of possession that, when passed down, is designated to be kept in the family of origin.

So, for example, if I choose them, I would promise they would be passed down on our side of the family. I would not sell them or give them to my spouse. In this sense, the possessions may "live forever," giving a sense of the continuity of a family that lasts many generations after individual members have passed on.

One of the ways these valuable connecting heirlooms are imbued with meaning and value is to make sure that the story that goes with them is relayed from one generation to the next. You may want to write down the history of objects and put it into a special book so that it will not be forgotten. You may print this story from a computer and pass it on to each child and even grandchild so that many will know and remember the stories. Pictures—or even a video—of the items may accompany the narrative for those who wish to take it a step further.

Less secure but equally important are oral histories passed from parent to children. These are important because they allow the child to write down the story if the parent has not already done so, and because they provide the parent a chance to enjoy the passing of stories down to children. Just as so many other details around the inheritance taboo are so often neglected or forgotten, this telling of the story of heirlooms may not be done as completely as it should.

When we ask why it wouldn't be, the answer is always the same: To have the forethought to write down the history of the objects requires accepting that we will not live forever. It means facing the end without self-delusion. It is easy *not* to make doing this a priority, and to do it haphazardly and incompletely when we finally do.

It follows then—in the same way trying to talk about one's inheritance wishes directly with children is much more easily done when we are in good health and of clear mind—that it's best to pass on the stories related to heirlooms when we are healthy and able to make it a meaningful family experience. We can do this when the object is being used or worn. It doesn't even need to be put in the context of inheritance, just a sharing of the family history so that the objects will be appreciated by all. Ideally, it should be written down, so that facts and the parent's associations to the item are clear.

In the same vein, the passing down of one's values is another common part of the inheritance process. Along with designating certain possessions we want to end up with a specific child, followed by the history of these objects, when significant, we may also prepare comments, stories, reminders, and even specific speeches to each heir regarding values through which we want to be remembered.

This passing on of values has been more widely practiced in recent years as a result of the ease of producing video recordings. In addition, the advent of converting video recordings to digital media has given us a relatively easy and widely available technology for preserving this kind of information. To be able to watch your mother on a videotape or computer disk any time you want, as she reminds you of certain important spiritual or philosophical values, can keep her beliefs and spirit very much alive and close to your heart.

We no longer have any reason for our children or extended family not to be able to recall the images, mannerisms, and words of a departed loved one. But these kinds of media productions require forethought. They require a willingness to accept that none of us will live forever. Children or relatives should be encouraged to take the time to capture the parents, preferably when parents are still in good health.

As a parent or grandparent, think about what values you wish to pass on to your family. Would you like to make a videotape that expresses these values directly to your children and grandchildren, nieces and nephews? Would you prefer to make a voice recording only? How about a digital movie that your family can watch at any time on their computer?

Or would you perhaps like to gather your family around you on a special occasion and tell them directly how you feel? If you have no interest in telling your family what you want them to remember in the way of values, life lessons, or your hopes for their future, think about *why* you don't want to take advantage of this opportunity.

EXAMPLE OF ESTRANGEMENT AND INHERITANCE

Earlier I gave a personal example of how I was quite satisfied to sustain the images, memories, and connection to my father using only a few of his possessions. In a similar vein, sometimes a few personal items from our childhood turn out to be as important as any amount of money that we may inherit. For those who end up being estranged from one or both parents, an inheritance of any type may be the last thing that he or she ever expected.

Here is a story sent to me by a woman who had given up on her parents and been out of contact with them for decades. She ended up receiving an inheritance that revived old resentments and forced her to consider whether or not she would even accept it.

"Back around 1995, I had not had any contact with my parents for about twenty years. I'd been through psychotherapy and decided around 1975 that it was in my best interests to cut off all contact. And my parents really never tried to find me or contact me—that was a big, ironic hurt in itself.

"So I came home from work one day (I think it was 1995) and had received a letter that communicated to me that both parents were now dead. My father had died a while earlier and left everything to my mother. Now my mother had also died. My mother's will left something to me, and the lawyers were trying to determine if I was still alive so they could get the inheritance to me. My parents had taken out an insurance policy on me back in my childhood. I had been in touch with the insurance company a few years earlier—trying to get the cash value out of the policy. I am an only child and both parents were only children, so there were no family disputes surrounding any of this.

"My mother had left most of her money to charities, particularly those that had helped her in her final years. But about 15 percent of the total was to come to me. So suddenly, all the old wounds were opened up again. I had to question whether I would accept the money at all, given my bitter feelings toward my parents. Ultimately, I decided that it felt like taking reparations for all the hurt they had done to me early in life. I decided to accept the money and do something significant with it.

"I asked my attorney to handle the entire process for me in order to keep my current personal information private. He let me use his office one night to go through the boxes and remove the few things that had personal meaning for me. The most important thing I inherited were my baby pictures—photos of me in infancy and childhood. I had wanted them for years and could picture the scrapbooks vividly. Those photos meant more to me than the money. So with the money, I paid off my mortgage. I now owned the home free and clear. That was significant and memorable to me."

This story nicely illustrates that even when you have suffered irreparable damage from your parents and had no contact for many years, something good may still come from whatever inheritance may be left to you.

Connecting to your childhood from early pictures becomes a chance to get a fuller sense of the continuity of your life. And money left to you by parents you have given up on becomes a chance to make yourself more financially secure. The price, however, is that you've got to be willing to go through the pain of revisiting some of those early unpleasant memories. In the above example, the woman was willing to do this, and benefited from it.

Now that we've looked at the meaning of possessions, the next task is for us to begin the actual process of dividing them. I will take you step by step through an outline of this process in the next chapter.

CHAPTER 11
DIVIDING THE GOODS
WITHOUT THE "SHOULDS"

If the last chapter didn't make it crystal clear, let me say it again: One of the psychological realities of inheritance is that decisions around personal property are often more challenging than those around titled property. You must not assume the division of personal property is a trivial matter, even if the possessions themselves are of limited monetary value.

I have reiterated that how siblings experience the process of division can have serious consequences on their future relationships. Because of this, it's a good idea to have given the process some thought and to have a systematic plan for how it is to unfold. In this chapter, I will take you through an organized approach that covers the basics. It emphasizes the need to keep real-time, precise records of agreements and choices made. But it's also meant to be flexible in dealing with disagreements as they arise and does not assume there's any one way that everyone "should" deal with their emotions.

One aspect of this planning is a method for dealing with the disagreements and conflicts that are likely to arise. When all siblings have input into resolving conflicts, they are more likely to agree and adhere to them. They are also more likely to feel the decisions are fair.

For the purposes of discussing distribution, we will assume that any items specified by the parent for an individual child and *already physically handed to the child* have been set aside and are no longer at issue. But this does *not* include the parent telling the child, "I want you to have my emerald necklace," but not actually giving it to the child. Verbally expressed intentions *that are not written in the will* may become a hotbed of sibling contention and is something we will discuss below.

We will also assume that, aside from any specified items, the parent's instruction was a typical one: "Divide my possessions equally among all children." We will assume that all sibs are able to meet at one location on a designated day and time to begin the distribution process.

Further, we will assume that a will or trust existed and that one of the sibs or close family members was made executor of the trust. For example, a son-in-law who is an accountant or attorney may be chosen by the parent. The executor is responsible for organizing and guiding the process, hopefully with input and consideration of other sibs involved. Remember, however, that most trusts give a great degree of power to the executor to administer the distribution.

The executor's word is final. While the good part of this is that it may keep sibs from endless arguing and thus results in decisions being made in a more timely manner, the downside is that the sib the parent chose to be the executor is in a prime position for criticism from other sibs for those same decisions. It's a powerful role to play within the family, around an issue of such importance, especially during a time when all are as emotionally vulnerable as they mourn their loss. And if one sib is chosen instead of all being designated as coexecutors, it may revive old feelings of being favored by the parent.

Because of this vulnerability, the role may seduce the executor to present himself in a controlling, dictatorial manner, alienating sibs and family members. This makes it a role that is ripe for potential relationship problems, as this is the person who will most likely be blamed when there are disappointments or when decisions made are deemed "unfair" by others. And this is the same person likely to not be given much credit by sibs no matter how well he executes his duties. In that way, the executor must derive any satisfaction from his role in knowing that he's doing what his parent would have wanted to the best of his ability. Waiting for sibs to be appreciative of the efforts is usually a futile exercise.

POWER AND CONTROL ISSUES

The power the executor of the trust wields will mean control over the following considerations directly related to dividing the possessions:

- The dates, times, and places of the distribution
- The ground rules for the distribution
- Determining distribution options and consequences
- Control over which items are considered as individual, pair, or group choices and which items will be given special consideration because of their perceived value by all involved
- Keeping and distributing an ongoing record of all choices made by all participants
- Deciding on the time limit allowed for each choice to be made as well as how long the process will continue once the choosing process begins
- Determining who will be allowed to be included in the process to observe or assist, such as spouses or children
- Acting as the final arbiter as to issues of fairness and equality
- Confirming that all items are removed when the choosing is completed and determining under what terms any items not chosen will be distributed or discarded if not desired by family members

The executor needs to be especially aware of the sensitivities of siblings have about power and control issues. Because the executor is entrusted to manage the estate funds, he must make every effort to show that he's taking care of all the business related to ongoing expenses of the estate. He must, at the very least, be a competent manager of money and be able to assertively protect the estate from specious claims made by doctors, lawyers, banks, hospitals, social clubs, and friends and relatives of the deceased.

The person in this role must be organized and able to make decisions despite going through his own grieving. He must have a general knowledge of what is required to distribute the assets and not be afraid to consult experts in those areas where he has inadequate knowledge. Because none of the sibs may have the skills needed to manage the estate, outside consultants are sometimes designated by the executor. The executor, in other words, has the power to bring in an outside person to take over and oversee the process, if for any reason he believes this is necessary. This action, of course, may lead to considerable expense that would otherwise be unnecessary.

One way the executor may demonstrate sensitivity to sibs is by eliciting, at each stage of the way, their input. But it isn't enough simply to make a pretense of considering the others. The executor must show that he is able to establish a policy based on the feedback sibs give him.

So, for example, the executor may ask the others how they think certain items should be grouped. Should two nightstands go as a pair (one choice) or individually (as two choices)? Should a pair of candlesticks go as one item or two? Should a headboard that was made to match a bed frame be included with the bed or be separate? This kind of detail, which may seem relatively minor, must be resolved or it becomes an area of potential bitterness.

If a sib wasn't chosen as the executor, he may try to exercise control by refusing to comply with the rules the executor sets up. While the executor has the final word, sibs may sabotage his authority by refusing to comply with deadlines or meeting times, or by not performing tasks assigned to them in a timely or competent manner. Passive-aggressive behavior (showing anger or hostility through a passive, indirect behavior) may include making "mistakes" when they finally do comply, so that the process is interrupted and slowed down, if they believe it may suit their own interests.

So, for example, the executor sib may give his sister an instruction to pay for the parent's car that she wishes to buy from the estate by a certain date. The sister refuses to comply with the deadline, dragging out the process until she feels ready to send the check. Since legal expenses will dilute the net value of what all sibs inherit, the passive-aggressive sib may have figured out she is likely to get away with her stalling tactic without any literal price to pay. But this doesn't mean she won't anger her sibs, causing the inheritance process to be more disagreeable than is necessary.

Often, when confronted, the person will deny any conscious intent to subvert the process and give an excuse as to why he didn't comply. The best way to know whether the passive-aggressive behavior is consciously intended is to use your knowledge of the person's past behavior with you. If you can decipher a history of the same sort of passive aggression, you can usually be assured this is a personality trait rather than a one-time mistake.

Besides the passive-aggressive refusal to honor the authority that is inherent in the executor role, sibs may also subvert the process through direct lying about what they have touched or taken of the parent's possessions. Sibs may hide, steal, or sell items without informing the others.

Resentments may spring forth in the form of a rationalization: "I never got what I deserved because Mom always favored them—the only way to make things more equal now is for me to take a few things. They will never even know these things are missing, so what will it hurt?"

Like it or not, you may see a side of your sibs that you never wanted to believe existed. These greedy, dishonest, and manipulative behaviors surface as current anger, past resentments, and the pain of loss combine to create a toxic potion that dilutes personal ethics and is poisonous to sibling relationships.

All of these actions are meant to exert power over the process indirectly. We resort to these when we perceive that we can't influence or control the process more directly. And all of these behaviors may cause sibs to become so bitter that they lose all trust and cooperation with each other. It is exactly this kind of rancor that families fear and that makes dealing more directly with inheritance issues such a taboo. Talk about your potential for a vicious cycle!

FAIRNESS REVISITED

In Chapter 5, we initiated the discussion on fairness. Now we must return to it. One of the things all sibs care about is whether or not the distribution process is fair. Remember, the concern for fairness is not just the fear of losing out on an object deemed valuable. It also involves the mental "scorecard" of resentments—the revival of all past issues between siblings as to whether they have been treated fairly by the others.

> **!** Because of this, everyone involved will overvalue fairness and equality. This means they will be given more weight than they ought to because we will remember childhood, adolescent, and even adult instances of perceived unfairness or inequality. We may express these long-held emotions during the distribution of parental belongings.

The most logical and impartial way of determining the order for choosing various items is to draw numbers from a hat or use an equally impartial way. While the eldest may believe that she "ought" to be granted priority to choose first, sensitivity to the others means the eldest should no longer gain the "elder favor" that she may have enjoyed growing up.

A systematic way to distribute the goods without a lot of "shoulds" is for each sib to choose one item from the pool of available items, taking continual turns until all items have been chosen or passed by. The pool of eligible items may be further broken down by room (if in the parent's house) or by category, so that all sibs are aware of exactly what is up for grabs and what will be put aside for later choosing. After sibs discuss various options for determining the way they might proceed, the executor has the final say as to the one selected. For any disagreements that may arise along the way, the executor is *always* the one whose opinion rules.

Each sib should have the opportunity to walk through the house where the possessions are and make notes as to what they are interested in. At this stage the executor, with input from sibs, should decide which items will be set aside for choosing at another time, assuming that there may be more than can be distributed at one time. It's also the time to decide which items will be chosen as pairs or groups. Sibs can then make notes, so they know exactly what their choices will include and what must be chosen separately.

One fairness issue is whether or not to consider the perceived monetary value when choosing. In other words, sibs might decide that all items valued over $500 should be tabulated and equally distributed. Or they may decide that each one will have a choice without regard to the perceived monetary value. This is clearly an easier way to go if all can agree.

It's possible for parents to believe they are being fair when a stamp collection, valued at $10,000, is given to one child and the same amount of cash is given to another child. The stamp collection may have appreciated in value over the years so that a situation known as "unintentional inequality" is set up. This term was coined by attorneys Barry Fish and Les Kotzer in their book *The Family Fight: Planning to Avoid It.* They make the argument that if the parent does not periodically review the will and make alterations as needed to deal with this kind of appreciating gift, unintentional inequality may result, leading to feelings of unfairness among sibs.

It's useful to have a discussion and address any feelings about fairness that sibs are having *before* the choosing process begins. This discussion may be part of a larger discussion about ground rules for choosing, as well as any issues that need to be resolved before the choosing begins.

ANNOUNCING THE GROUND RULES

Once sibs have managed to meet on the appointed date and place of distribution and all are ready to begin the process of distribution, the first order of business is for the executor to announce the ground rules. As part of refreshing the memories of those involved, it may be useful for the executor to read a copy of the actual trust document, which outlines the powers of the executor. The ground rules will include the method of distribution and limitations.

For example, your ground rules might be something like this: Each sib will have one choice in turn, with the order of choosing to be determined randomly. The process of choosing in the established order will continue until all items are chosen or until a predetermined time is met. Each sib will have five minutes to make her choice. If an item is not chosen within that time period, she would be warned and another two minutes will be given. If she fails to choose within that warning period, she will lose her choice. Bathroom breaks may be taken and will not be counted against one's time limit.

Try to think ahead one or two choices, so you can make your choice without undue deliberation. All choices are final unless a crucial piece of information is revealed after the choice that renders the choice to be made out of inadequate or false information. The final determination as to any choices that will be voided is up to the executor.

The ground rules include which rooms or types of items are open for being chosen out of the total universe of possessions. If a large home with many items collected over a lifetime is up for grabs, it makes sense to do the choosing by groups, so that all sibs can more easily keep in mind the possibilities and so that very different types of items are not in the mix together.

For example, you might determine that all jewelry will be chosen as a separate category, or that all kitchen items, including pots and pans, will be chosen as a separate group. Another group that is easy to keep separate would be bed linens.

It is very important that it be clear to all sibs exactly what can be chosen and what will be put aside for later consideration. The job of the executor is to make sure a sib knows that he or she has made an "out of the universe" choice should he or she forget in the pressure or excitement of the moment.

ANNOUNCING PRIOR CLAIMS

One aspect of the pre-choosing agenda should be the declaration by each sib as to any prior claims to specific items belonging to the estate. Over the course of the parent's life, each child may have given gifts to the parent. At the same time, the parent may have told the child that either these same gifts or different items will go to the child upon the parent's death.

This can be a tricky area, making for heated discussions among sibs before the choosing process has even begun because it requires a willingness to trust the word of the sib making a claim. One sib may say he gave a piece of art to the parent and that it is now his, that he has a right to take it back. Another may say she bought specific outdoor plants for the parent many years ago and is now making a claim they are hers. One brother claims Mom "promised" him the piano that has been in the family for thirty years.

It is easy for other sibs to question (both internally and aloud) why possession was not taken earlier of items claimed if they were so important to the sib: "Did Mom *really* want you to have that item? Did she *really* say it was yours but never write it down in her will or anywhere else? And why didn't she at least mention it to me or anyone else?"

As long as the items being peremptorily claimed do not hold too much value to other sibs, it may not be an issue of contention. It may also be acceptable when each sib has something they are claiming to be theirs and so the others feel it is relatively fair. But when two sibs each believe a promise was made to them for the same item, an argument may ensue that colors the choosing process that is to follow.

During this announcing of prior claims phase, you can avoid both short- and long-term resentments by adopting a more encompassing perspective by asking yourself, "Does this item really matter to me? Or would it mean a lot more to my brother to go ahead and let him have it without argument?" This may not only result in a quick resolution of prior claims made on items, but make the other sibs appreciate the gesture and be more inclined to take you seriously when another issue comes up further in the disposition process.

Another way to say this: Sometimes a means to resolve disputes is by avoiding them to begin with. Do you really care if your brother makes a claim on the piano that you can't play and don't even want? Do you care if your sister makes a claim on some plants or a piece of art?

Resolution tip: Go ahead and give your sibs what they claim as long as the argument they are making to back up the claim sounds reasonably plausible and there is no information that you have that would directly contradict the claim or you know you don't want the item anyway.

WHO IS INCLUDED?

Another issue that must be considered before the choosing begins is whether the sibs wish to have anyone else assisting them in making their choices. Some families believe that this is a closed and private encounter, one in which no one besides the immediate children should participate. Much of this will have to do with the history of family alliances and feelings about spouses and relatives.

When one sib has a spouse and the others don't, for example, it may be perceived that the spouse's assistance will give unfair advantage over the others. This is more likely to be the case when the sibs feel competitive with one another. Since the time limit imposed on all makes for a degree of pressure to make a "good" choice, there is some element of truth to the notion that two minds may work better than one in decision making.

For example, my two brothers were reluctant to allow my wife of more than twenty-six years, whom they both love as a sister, to sit at the table during the process. They thought she might give me an "unfair advantage" in helping make my choices. It was as if something might be taken away from them if I had this "advantage" of a second mind to help make choices. Finally, however, they realized that her twenty-six years by my side and being an integral part of our family entitled her to be part of the process—but not until after some discussion.

The case could be made that children of any of the sibs should not even in be in the house while the distribution takes place. In this way, should the sibs begin arguing with each other or say things that are hurtful, no children would witness such a negative interaction among family.

But the other side of the coin here is that children at least somewhere in the house or on the grounds might attenuate any loss of emotional control by sibs, knowing their children are going to hear them if things get out of control.

How about girlfriends? Should they be included? What about an uncle or aunt who may be curious to see what happens? Or close family friends? The easiest way to decide who attends is to ask whether the person is going to be actively involved in the process of choosing—either for themselves or for a sib. If they are, it makes sense to consider having them. If not, it probably doesn't.

LET THE CHOOSING BEGIN

After the executor explains the ground rules and peremptory claims for specific items have been made and resolved, it's time to begin the choosing of personal property. The executor should be keeping track of the claims made and their disposition, preferably on a laptop computer.

A modified spreadsheet may be constructed with the names of each sibling heading a column in order of choosing. Each choice made by each sib would be noted across from a brief description of the item itself. Here is an example:

EXAMPLE OF PERSONAL PROPERTY DISTRIBUTION LOG

ITEM	John (first)	Mary (second)	Mark (third)
Dining room oak table with lazy Susan	Choice #1 2:37 P.M.		
Portrait of Mom at desk in living room		Choice #1 2:37 P.M.	
Silver candlesticks (taken with him)			Choice #1 2:40 P.M.
Silverware matched set for 12 (taken with him)	Choice #2 2:47 P.M.		
Living room couch		Choice #2 3:05 P.M.	
Den sectional furniture			Choice #2 3:10 P.M.
Dry bar cabinet in dining room	Choice #3 3:16 P.M.		

Creating this kind of simple table is a good way for all sibs to re-member what was chosen on each turn without each of them having to keep a separate list, which detracts from moving the process along. A copy of the entire table may then be sent as an e-mail attachment to each sibling by the executor upon completion.

One way to have a more cooperative process is for each sib to show interest in the choices the others make. Usually, this is not hard to do, since more than one participant will desire many items. The process can be made a bit lighthearted, as exclamations such as "Good choice, Johnny! We knew you always liked that mirror" can reinforce the sib's choice, making him feel satisfied and less on guard that he has over-looked something more desirable.

Reinforcing sibs' choices also taps into their early need for sibling approval. You might not think approval over a choice like this matters much to adult sibs who are feeling competitive with one another. But no matter what the age, the fact that the approval is coming from sibs makes it more significant and lends an air of cooperation and family co-hesiveness to the proceedings.

Keeping it lighthearted is also a useful way to counter the darker side of the reality actually occurring. No matter how much the sibs may feel some excitement at the prospect of receiving certain objects that they have long liked and wanted, the reality is that they are taking over their dead parent's possessions. For some, the weight of this realization will result in waves of emotion passing through them during the course of the choosing process.

> Memories may flood the mind, as we make the connections be-tween the object and parent again and again. This results in a fairly intense emotional experience for many of us, one that is more powerful than we might have anticipated. This will especially be true if the choosing process lasts many hours with little or no break or when there is enough to divide that more than one session is required.

MANAGING AND RESOLVING CONFLICTS

Unless you come from a passive and nonconfrontational family, in which everyone gets along by never raising their voices about anything, plan on there being some tension and disagreements. This is even more likely if there are a lot of items to choose from and a number of hours to complete the distribution. There are just too many issues to argue about and too much material from the past to make itself felt in the present, especially with the backdrop of vulnerability from grieving.

Resolving conflicts requires listening closely to your sib's position. Your sibs will test you to see if, during this stressful grieving time, the same old emotional buttons that have always been able to provoke you are still in operation. They will not necessarily do this consciously—but they will do it at some point.

The more upset about some issue a sib is, the more she will try to work you up into the same emotional state. And because—besides a parent or spouse—your sibs are the very best at being able to probe your weak spots, you will have to stay on your emotional toes!

Managing and resolving conflicts will be easier if:

1. Sibs realize *and can identify* how the past is coloring the present interactions around inheritance distribution;
2. Sibs can talk about their feelings of loss and find positive ways to connect through their shared grieving before distribution begins;
3. Sibs acknowledge that the easier they can make it for one another, the easier it will be for themselves;
4. A family ritual, such as sharing a meal or taking a walk, can be practiced when tension gets to a level that angry disputes are on the edge of breaking out;
5. Sibs feel that it is safe to bring up disagreements and discuss them and that the executor will do her best to honor the majority opinion;
6. The executor is not using the situation for her own power needs;

7. There is a basic sense of good faith among sibs that will override petty jealousies, envy, and competitiveness;

8. Outside the immediate circle, other family members are willing to stay out of the process so as not to complicate it;

9. Sibs are able to remember the long-term foundation of their relationships rather than focus too heavily on winning a short-term victory; and

10. Emotions related to the grieving process are able to be contained so that volatility between sibs is curbed.

Here is a sample of potential conflicts and ways of resolving them.

Conflict: Sibs feel the executor is being "unfair" in his making ground rules, choices, etc.

Example: The executor's brother wants the heirloom candlesticks, which ought to be chosen as a pair and kept together, not as separate items. Despite ardent discussion as to the rationale behind keeping them together as a pair—that one won't look right on a table, that candlesticks *always* go as a pair, etc.—the executor decides to separate them. His thinking is that if one is lost, the other will be with another sib, thus ensuring that at least one remains and also that making them two items means more than one sib can possess and enjoy one of them.

Now, it is clear from the order of choosing as the proceedings begin that he personally will gain by being able to choose one of them once the other one is chosen. He, of course, doesn't point this out or indicate that this fact has anything to do with his thinking. Despite this decision being self-serving, the sibs must simply accept it and move on.

Resolution Tip: If the choosing has already begun, ask for a time-out from being on the clock and bring up the issue to all sibs. Explain what it is you feel is unfair and why. Ask other sibs, including the executor, what they think. If other sibs agree with you, ask the executor to reconsider the decision. Then accept the executor's final decision and move on. Use the strength of your reaction to gain a moment of insight: Notice how attached you are to your position. Use this awareness to remember what really matters to you. In doing so, you will escape the sense of needing to have it your way.

Conflict: Resentment from the past begins to surface, as you notice you are making snide comments to your sibs having to do with their ending up with "better" possessions. While you realize that the luck of the draw meant you were selecting last, you've had plenty of choices with which you could have picked what they did. Your choices seem to be colored by an underlying sense of dissatisfaction. You begin to notice you are feeling some disgust with the whole distribution process. You also realize this is irrational and are able to see it must be coming from somewhere else. But where? And what to do?

Example: "Ah yes, I felt this same feeling back when Mom gave each of them a more expensive gift for their birthdays than she gave me." Or: "This reminds me of how Dad always favored Johnny—he got the new Callaway golf clubs and I only got some crappy knockoffs."

Resolution Tip: See if you can identify when you last felt this same way when your sibs were involved. Was it a family contest of some sort? A party or competition in which you thought you got second prize? Or perhaps a family event in which you were not given the attention of your sibs? If you are able to see a connection between the past and the present, immediately try to put into a sentence what resentment is being revived.

Conflict: Guilt-tripping by family members or friends out of anger at not getting something they want. This may be interpreted as righteous indignation expressed through attempts at shaming the other into complying with a request or desire.

Example: Before the distribution process begins, a daughter-in-law comes by the parent's house to pick up an item that she believes is hers. It's a card table that had been at the house for some time. One of the sibs who happens to be there at the time objects to this, claiming that the table is not hers and that she can't take it. He says that it was *his* table, that *he* left it there. She gets upset and says to him, "Your mother would have been ashamed of your behavior for not giving me what was mine!"

Resolution Tip: Invoking the dead person's imagined judgment on the behavior of family members is a low blow. Just don't do it. It is a barely disguised attempt to shame the family member into giving you what you want. Resist the temptation to engage in a shouting match with the others. Refuse to stoop down to the same level. Family members should realize that this kind of plea is not going to get them what they want. Especially when everyone is still grieving, it is simply hurtful to tell others how the parent would have felt about anyone's behavior.

Conflict: Disagreement among sibs regarding what is acceptable to give away to a family member; how the raw emotions of mourning color judgment on the day of the funeral; and how there is a right time and a wrong time for a relative to request possessions of the parent, regardless as to what is convenient for the relative.

Example: After the funeral ceremony, everyone congregates at the parent's home for a reception. One of those attending is an out-of-town granddaughter-in-law who is only visiting for a couple of days. A rather large number of people are mingling in the house and the backyard. With so many people wandering freely around the house, one of the sibs has sequestered the parent's jewelry for safekeeping.

The granddaughter-in-law asks one of the sibs if it's okay to "take a look" at the books in the library. The sib takes this to mean she may want to take a few books with her, and he has no objection to this. But he says nothing to the other sibs, who feel differently about it than he did. The woman helps herself to a handful of books, but as she is walking out with them, another sib stops her and asks what she is doing. She says, "Your brother told me it was okay." This sib protests and tells her no objects are to leave the house. Hoping to have had a few books to remember her grandmother by, she is hurt and angry. When it's clear that she isn't going to get them on her terms, she stomps out of the house.

In the same vein, and only a short time later, the deceased parent's brother wants an old portrait of his mother. He, too, becomes angry when told that nothing is going to leave the house. In addition, despite his poor sense of timing, they have no intention of giving him this old and valuable portrait.

A heated argument arose among the sibs from these two incidents. Not only did it make things strained for the rest of the evening, but they continued to revive this issue for weeks after. It was difficult for the sib who felt he was only trying to be generous and thoughtful by allowing items to be taken to understand that the other two sibs didn't see it that way. They felt it was far more important not to be giving things away before they had even had a chance to deal with the death and burial of their mother.

Resolution Tip: Establish a policy regarding the taking of any of the parent's items from the premises—both for you yourselves and for any other relatives. Especially when a reception will follow at the home of the parent, and items will be in plain view, sibs need to be clear regarding whether they want anyone to be able to request and/or take any items.

Relatives and friends need to be sensitive to the "vulture factor," which is the premature or inappropriate grasping for the money or possessions of the dead parent. Sibs may view relatives as wanting to take something for the right reasons but *at the wrong time.* And, because of their own emotional state, it is this poor timing that sibs will remember—not the relatives' good intentions to have an object to remember their parent.

Never ask for anything on the day of the funeral, as sibs are likely to interpret this as terribly poor timing. The issue here was that what was convenient for the granddaughter-in-law and acceptable to one sib was viewed as insensitive and unacceptable by the other sibs. The books themselves were of sentimental value only and probably would have been given to her *when the sibs were ready.* But this was the day the sibs had just buried their mother—definitely not the time to start ransacking her house simply for the convenience of out-of-town relatives.

Conflict: In attempting to begin the process of getting rid of junk possessions that have been in the parent's house for years but are not directly related to the parent who has died, an adult child may gather together old files that are irrelevant or objects that he believes will have no value to anyone. He begins this process only a week after the parent has died by purposely tossing out the *least emotional* material—objects he doesn't think anyone else could possibly object to. But he has assumed that what he considers to be trash will be of no value to his sibs. And he finds out this isn't true.

Example: Very old checkbooks and ledgers, as well as business files that are long irrelevant were all thrown into a large plastic bag. They were records kept by the parent only because they had belonged to her spouse, who had died five years previously. She had not been able to go through and toss out any paperwork that had no value. But when the sib told his executor brother about doing what he believed was a service to all of them, another sib told him he might want some of these old records. The objecting sib methodically picked through the large plastic garbage bag filled with paper, checking to make sure that it contained nothing of value.

Resolution Tip: In the same way that some sibs are not ready to see anything leave the premises by way of relatives or friends while they are still mourning their loss, they may not be able to part with even old payment records, twenty-year-old canceled bank checks, or cheap objects that at any other time they would view as trash. They are still too numbed by their mourning to part with anything, no matter how meaningless it may seem. Because of this numbness, it's best to remember that it may take awhile before sibs are ready to deal with parting with objects. Again, what one sib may be ready to part with, another may not be.

Remember that when people are mourning, many are not ready to do *anything* for a while, no matter how small or inconsequential it may seem. The problem is that important decisions regarding estate disposition don't wait for the right psychological or emotional moment. Many decisions need to be made and actions taken soon after the death of a parent—despite the fact that family members are just beginning their grieving.

Depending on your personality and coping defenses, like the sib in the example above, you may want to dig in and get the process moving so that you can get past the ugliness of death as soon as possible. If this is your style, remember that your sibs may not deal with the trauma in the same fashion. You need to be respectful of their different styles of coping with loss.

Now we move to the next chapter, in which we deal more directly with the process of mourning and grieving.

CHAPTER 12
MANAGING GRIEF AND
FINDING RELIEF

The models of grieving that psychology has to offer will not prepare you for the depth of sorrow and loss you will feel when your parent dies. But having a map of the stages that typically occur may help you navigate the strong emotions when they arise, making room for them with less fear and apprehension. Knowing what to expect may also help you respect the need to be careful of your decision making during a period of mourning and grief.

Since there are many resources online and in print available for dealing with grieving, I will offer only the barest of outlines here. In describing typical grieving reactions, it will be more apparent how the death of a parent affects your reactions to family members during the inheritance process.

> **[!]** My premise is simple: If you know that after your parent dies, everything you are thinking, saying, and doing is likely to be exaggerated and magnified, *this knowledge alone* may help you temper your responses. It can help prevent the kind of overreaction that is so often responsible for splitting families apart. And it can help avoid the kinds of toxic behaviors that are likely to occur when we are feeling empty, lost, angry, and confused.

First, let's define the terms. *Bereavement* means to be deprived by death. *Mourning* is the inner process you go through when you feel this deprivation. *Grief* is the outward, visible sign of mourning, made up of physical and emotional symptoms we experience following the death of a loved one. It is commonly held in psychology that if you don't grieve at the time of death or shortly after, you may end up with emotional and/or physical problems later on. The term for this is "complicated bereavement."

Grieving is not limited to the death of a loved one. We also experience it with the loss or change in a living situation, either by choice or by outside circumstances. For example, you will grieve the loss of your home if it is suddenly destroyed by fire, tornado, or earthquake. You may also grieve a change in living situation, such as moving from a home to an apartment or assisted-living situation. The loss of a pet, job, girlfriend, or marriage—or anything else that you are emotionally attached to—may cause some form of grieving, even if of relatively minor intensity and duration. Generally, the deeper the attachment to the lost person or object, the stronger your reaction will be.

STAGES OF GRIEVING

A theory of the stages of grieving was made popular by the pioneering work of psychiatrist Elisabeth Kübler-Ross in 1969. In the intervening thirty years, many health-care professionals have since questioned whether all grieving people must go through these stages and have raised other questions related to her model.

Some would say that you don't even really begin grieving until *after* you have gone through these stages. They view grieving as a complicated, multidimensional, and individual process that can't be captured in five stages. For some of the problematic issues that have been raised regarding Kübler-Ross's theory and research, see the Web site http://www.bereavement.org/elm_st_article.htm. Because her model is so widely known, I will briefly identify the stages and add some comments as to what may be experienced at each stage.

1. Denial: "No, not me, it cannot be true."
This initial reaction to loss may last a few hours, days, or even weeks. The mind cannot take in the full shock of what has happened, so you

become numb, as if the death has not yet registered. This numbing allows for taking care of practical arrangements around the funeral and various other social and legal obligations related to the death.

As a few days pass, you may begin to experience a yearning for your parent. For at least the first month or so, you will find it difficult to concentrate on everyday affairs, work, or family. You will find yourself spending a lot of time in your mind remembering the final scenes with your parent, final conversations, and anything else that seems relevant to the end of your parent's life. You will feel like you're walking around in a daze, doing things absentmindedly. You will ruminate over the kinds of things you think you "should" have said or done to help that you didn't. You may become obsessed by certain scenes or conversations, unable to get them out of your head. And you may blame yourself if you believe you didn't do something that could have prolonged your parent's life.

You will try to find meaning in small things your parent said or did toward the end. And you will replay numerous scenes in your mind related to your relationship with your parent, some of them taking you back through your childhood. Playing back these scenes from the past may bring up strong emotion, as the reality of the death begins to sink in. Your first thoughts in the morning will be about death and loss. And your last thoughts as you try to fall asleep will be the same. You will struggle to let in the full force of the agony of your loss.

2. Anger: "Why me?"

Strong emotion will begin to surface: sobbing at your loss, emptiness, and anger at being separated from your parent. While anger is common with the tragic death in midlife of a spouse, or a child or adolescent who is suddenly killed in an accident or by disease, it is not necessarily an emotion that you will experience with the death of a parent who has lived a full life and who did not die suddenly. This is even more likely to be true when the parent was dealing with pain and anguish from disease and where the death was viewed—both by the parent and children—as a release from further suffering.

Those who have a strong fear of abandonment will feel anger at the parent for what they believe has been done to them: "How could you leave me to have to manage the world on my own, without you?" At a deeper and usually unconscious level, many feel anger at being forced to face their *own* fear of death through dealing with the death of their parent.

3. Bargaining: "Yes, me, but . . . "

Here we try to come to terms with the death by trying to undo it. Our bargaining may not even be entirely conscious. You might have thoughts that you would exchange your own life if only the other could live. Again, this stage may be more predominant when there is a tragic death rather than when a parent who has lived a full life dies.

One form this stage may take is feeling guilty that you haven't done everything you could have done to save your parent. "If only I hadn't overlooked what she was eating," or, "If only I had stayed on top of her doctors to be more diligent." I have seen over and over again how adult children feel guilty for not somehow exerting a power they believe they have to change the condition of their parent. When I inquire closely, it turns out they usually have delusions of omnipotence, imagining they could have done something that really was out of their hands to influence. Some find it very difficult to accept that their best efforts were simply not enough to keep their parent alive. Bargaining may also include arguments with the dead parent about taking care of herself better or wishing you had just one more opportunity to say the things you never got to say.

4. Depression: "Yes, me."

At this point, the force of the loss is gradually being let in at a deeper level. Strong emotions make for volatile mood swings. You may feel emotionally raw and vulnerable to anything in your daily world that reminds you of the death. You may isolate yourself from friends for some time and find that your focus on your loss feels all-consuming, at least for a number of months. Loss of appetite, difficulty sleeping, and loss of interest in the activities that you usually find pleasurable are common. The whole world may be cast in a negative and depressive light, as you fixate on noticing the natural process of things as they arise, decay, and pass away in the living world.

You may find that dreams of your parent come up in various forms, from full-fledged nightmares replaying final scenes of death or the funeral to receiving loving guidance from your parent as to how to help yourself survive the loss. You may hear your parent's voice during the day when you want support, and attach yourself to objects that remind you of and keep you connected to the parent. Despair, confusion, longing, physical aching, and what may feel like unbearable pain may be experienced in waves that come and go.

The way you cope with this stage will have to do with your pattern of coping with past trauma in your life, your personality type, and your defenses. Some people will start binge eating while others will lose their appetite altogether for weeks at a time. Some will want to be in close contact with family members either in person, by phone, or e-mail. Others will want to isolate themselves and go through their grieving more privately. Some will want to escape the misery of death and dying by taking a trip as soon as the funeral and estate distribution are completed. Others will hunker down, staying close to home and spending a lot of time reflecting.

In this stage, when the agony of your loss seems unbearable, you may find yourself questioning the meaning of your own life and asking what values really matter to you. This evaluation may occur sometime down the line, when the strongest emotional waves have receded and you are able to begin thinking about your future. For some, this may lead to choices to end unproductive or unhappy careers. For others, it may lead to decisions to divorce or to radically rearrange their lives in some fashion. Some begin having fantasies of how their inheritance will finance these changes they want to make. Others imagine how they will escape their pain by indulging in pleasures they now think they can afford.

The knowledge that your parent is no longer here watching over you may bring insecurity about your ability to take care of yourself. But it may also bring a freedom to move in new directions. It begins to really sink in that you will never again enjoy the physical presence of your parent. This brings on renewed bouts of crying and anguish, which may be touched off by sentimental music, photos, or other associations to your parent.

This stage is the most difficult to negotiate not only because of the strong emotions you experience but also because you are often forced to deal with estate issues, including the distribution of personal property. At a time when it would be best to focus on grieving, decisions need to be made in dealing with your parent's estate. So it is easy for your grieving to influence decision making by making your decisions less rational and more emotionally tinged than they ought to be.

5. Acceptance and hope for the future: "It's okay."

Over the course of the first year or longer, the pain, sadness, and depression lessen. You begin to see your life more positively, returning to those activities that have brought you meaning and pleasure. Much of the rumination and obsession fade away; you are able to think of your parent without tears surfacing. You again have emotional energy to invest in those close to you. Normal patterns of sleep and diet return, and you are able to form a new inner relationship to your parent, with new ways of relating to him or her. You begin to forge a new direction, feeling a strength that comes from standing on your own feet without the parent there to nurture or guide you. You begin to enjoy activities again and can make plans and look forward without feeling lost, unbearably sad, or overwhelmed.

GRIEF WORK

Resolving your grief takes time and effort. The tendency for many is to believe that after a few months, as emotion quiets down, they have pretty much gone through the whole process of grieving. But losing a parent who has been in your life from the time you were born will not be completed in a few months, even if you had a strained relationship and didn't feel all that close.

The active process of grief work may be facilitated by taking some time each day to be open to whatever emotions may surface related to your loss. Some professionals suggest setting up a sanctuary or altar in your home, where each day you honor the memory of your parent. For example, I had a candle, incense, and a picture of my mother; for the first month following her death, each day I burned the candle and lit the incense while looking at the photo. I thought about some of the more pleasant and fulfilling experiences we'd shared. I began to actively "lock in" to my memory these times together, so that I could easily return to them anytime I wanted. I would then sit in meditation and focus my attention on any thoughts or feelings related to my loss.

Working with your grief means opening up to whatever your experience may be, no matter how powerful or unpleasant. It means allowing yourself to let the tears and sobbing come without interrupting yourself. This is somewhat easier for women to do in our culture than it is for men.

As part of active grief work, it is important to address any unfinished business you may have had with your parent. This means saying anything that needs to be said to be able to let your parent go — for example, unexpressed love, anger, resentment, regrets, or appreciations. While you can do a measure of this on your own, it's useful to have a skilled psychotherapist help you, as he or she is able to see things you may be avoiding, as well as help you connect past relationship dynamics with present unfinished business.

One way to express what is unfinished is to talk to your parent as if she is sitting next to you in an empty chair. If you want her to respond, you can switch chairs and let her answer. This two-chair dialogue method can be very powerful in helping you both say and hear back the kinds of things that help you feel more finished.

Another exercise is to write a letter to your parent. This is usually a more cerebral and less emotionally potent tool but can also help you express your deeper thoughts about the relationship. Some feel they can reflect more profoundly through writing than they can through speech.

It is therapeutic to gather with family members and share your experiences of your parent together. For those who also want more of a one-on-one situation, a spouse, trusted sib, or friend who knows you well may also be able to listen patiently as you talk about your parent. For some, speaking into a recorder has more emotion attached than writing their feelings. I found it surprisingly meaningful, for example, to play back my recording of the eulogy I gave at my mother's funeral service a number of times in the weeks following her death. Whatever tools you choose, the important thing is to express everything that needs to be expressed—without shame or guilt.

It's especially helpful to seek out a psychologist if you find that months are passing and you are unable to resume your normal activities or if you continue to have strong bouts of sobbing touched off by comments, pictures, memories, or anything else related to your parent.

> **!** Your family may go through a period of confusion and uncertainty, as each member struggles to deal with the loss of the parent. The family pattern will change, sometimes with one sibling stepping in to play the part of nurturer or disciplinarian. The family system will be unstable for a while, which means that you will have an opportunity to change the system if your sibs and others wish to create a new way of relating to each other. While this is not easy to do because of the power of past family dynamics, it's more possible when the system has been thrown into chaos, as it is with the death of a parent.

> **!** If siblings can manage to keep their communication open and be supportive of one another through their grieving, the deeper bonds they forge may help them preserve the family unit and help recreate a stable family system. If they allow disagreements over inheritance to dominate, they will lose this opportunity to forge the closer bond and instead create distance that may be difficult to undo. This is why the process of grieving is so relevant to dealing with inheritance issues. The family that can help each other deal with the common loss can also find ways to help each other through the division of the estate and personal possessions.

Grief work includes slowly creating a full picture of your parent, which means incorporating both strengths and weaknesses. To create this full picture, it is useful to review the course of your relationship beginning from the earliest times you can remember and continuing through all the stages of your life together. This is another one of those tasks that a psychologist can facilitate. She can help you sort out whatever is unresolved so that a more encompassing picture is possible.

What is called "informal conclusionary ritual" may also be used to help create an accurate memory picture of your parent. In addition to the more formal funeral service, family and friends may gather to share their experiences of the deceased. In their sharing, you create a more complete picture of the person who facilitates saying good-bye to the physical body, so you can create a new spiritual relationship. The idea is to create both a complete personality picture and also a literal memory picture. Be sure to look at photo albums that show early pictures of your parent, as well as photos and movies that show various ages in life. You want to remember your parent not only as he or she looked and behaved at the end of life, but when he or she was younger, healthy, and vibrant as well.

One example of a personal conclusionary ritual my family held was during the reception at my mother's home following the funeral service. Friends and family joined together to watch a video that had been made a few years earlier. In the video, one of our family members interviewed my mother, asking about her parents, upbringing, and many experiences from her life that described both her joyful and painful times.

Another form was for my brothers and me, along with other family members and close friends, to come together to play music. This music-making was something my mother always enjoyed listening to. It served to help us not only cope with our shared loss but also reinforce our continued bond with each other in a time of need. And, of course, it also kept us in touch with the rhythm of life.

Conclusionary ritual may also include periodic visits to the gravesite of your parent, setting up an altar in your home dedicated to your parent, and other projects such as creating photo albums or wearing or using certain personal possessions of your parent. For example, since my mother's death, I wear a silver bracelet that was hers; it keeps me close to her when I look at it.

Still another form would be to go back and read over any e-mail, notes, cards, and letters that your parent sent to you and to safely preserve them so that you may come back and refer to them in the future.

> **!** Active grief work is not going to be over in a few months. It will evolve over years, as you gain enough perspective on your relationship to allow the sentimental and idealized image that cloaks a more complete and balanced picture of who your parent really was in your life to fall away. The stable internalized image that results will help you connect spiritually with your parent.

You do not need to get caught in certain overly simplistic clichés that we tend to associate with the process of grieving. These include such sayings as, "Time heals all wounds," "You should be over it by now," and "You have to keep busy." There is no "right" way to grieve your loss—but using the kinds of tools I have shared here may definitely help you along the way. It's your responsibility to find the method that suits you, taking whatever time it may take you. You need *not* feel guilty when you choose not to accept someone else's idea of how you are supposed to deal with your loss.

> **!** A word of warning to those who are cognitively oriented and like to use their intellect to solve all problems: You will find that your intellect is unable to "figure out" the process of grieving. While the intellect will be useful in doing the suggested review of your history with your parent, as well as dealing with some of your unfinished business, it will not help you confront the emotions that are the primary stuff of grieving. Don't try to "solve" your grieving—just *experience* it.

Another aspect of grief work for you to consider is the "mop up" work that may be required to mend relationships with sibs and other family members after a difficult inheritance process. As the strong waves of emotion related to loss and grieving begin to recede, it is easier for sibs to gain some thoughtful perspective as to how these emotions made it easy for them to indulge in exaggerated responses to their sibs.

Time has a way of creating the necessary reflection for this to occur, leading to forgiveness. But if you avoid this repairing, time may instead deepen the resentment. Because of this, it is a good idea not to wait too long to begin mending the wounds that may have been inflicted when sibs and other family members were in the throes of their grieving but forced to address issues with property, money, and personal possessions before they were ready to.

Once the inheritance disposition process has been completed and sibs have had *at least a year* to make psychological and emotional adjustments that allow them to move on, they are more ready and able to apologize to each other for things that they may have said during the heat of the inheritance battle. They are more ready to accept whatever the outcome of the distribution may have been and realize that it isn't going to serve their own emotional needs to alienate their sibs for the rest of their lives.

Again, this may lead to mutual forgiveness. If it doesn't, the distance created may become hardened over time, resulting in exactly the kind of lifelong separation that is the history of the inheritance taboo. Or, at the least, it may create more emotionally distanced relationships than before the death. While you may continue to experience some bad feelings and all may not ever be the way you wish it would be, the important point here is to find a way to keep the connection to your sibs and not allow any bitterness to define the future of your relationship.

FORGING NEW DIRECTIONS

An important step in grief work is learning to nurture yourself. You do this through taking care of yourself in both large and small ways, from physically being kind and even pampering yourself to creating the environment around you that will sustain you emotionally. To begin nurturing yourself, you must first be willing to accept that your parents may not have been able to give you all the nurturing you wanted or deserved. If you resist this realization, it will be difficult to shift your energy and attention to caring for yourself. Instead, you will get lost in feeling resentment for what your parents and significant others never gave you.

Nurturing yourself means coming to realize that you can now, as an adult, give to *yourself* much of what you wanted from your parent. You can give yourself the approval for a job well done. You can be proud of your own accomplishments, whatever they may be. And you can give yourself the acceptance of your own uniqueness as a person that you wanted from your parent.

As your healing continues, let your friends and family know how they can help you. Some may initially shy away, as they will be unsure how to approach you or whether you even want contact with them. Don't be surprised if some around you are unable to give even a courteous "Sorry to hear about your loss." This avoidance is just another reflection of our culture's denial of death and awkwardness in dealing with it.

Nurturing yourself also means knowing who to turn to for comforting through your grieving. Men need to be able to ask their wife or girlfriend for emotional and physical comforting. When you trust a partner enough to be able to cry in her arms, you don't feel so lonely and isolated. You know someone is there who cares for you and who will help support you through the difficult time.

Nurturing yourself also means making sure you get proper nourishment, sleep, and physical exercise during the early months of grieving. This will help cope with the added stress of grieving and with the emotional exhaustion you will feel.

Assuming you end up with some money and personal possessions as a part of your inheritance, you will be faced with new choices as to how you want to spend this money. It's wise not to be in a hurry to make decisions about spending it. It's tempting, especially if you tend to be impulsive, to rush into a buying frenzy to help insulate yourself from the pain from your loss. Resist this temptation!

Instead, put the money into a savings account and take some time to deal with the emotional and psychological content that arises during grieving. You will make better decisions as to what you want to do with your inheritance if you are able to resist the temptation to blow some of it just to distract yourself from your pain.

Keep in mind that most who inherit modest amounts of money spend it within one year. Because they see it as a windfall, it is easy to justify spending it on luxuries or things that they have wanted for a long time but been unable to afford. But as we said at the beginning of this book, baby boomers who have had losses in the stock market or extended themselves on credit need to make careful decisions as to whether they use their inheritance to pay down their debt, help make up for losses, or quickly fritter it away on items that may make them feel good for a while but not really improve their financial condition.

As the months pass, you will find some relief. Don't be surprised to find yourself thinking of making some changes in your life. This is a normal part of the grieving process. *Death has a way of forcing us to see the things that we usually resist looking at.* Depending on your age when your parent dies, you may find yourself feeling some urgency to do some of the things you've thought about but never followed through with.

Those in their 40s, 50s, and 60s will be especially sensitized to the press of time. Your parent's death will remind you again and again how short your time is on this earth and how important it is to do those things that really matter to you and that bring meaning to your life.

Don't be afraid to let this keener awareness of the shortness of life push you into making plans and taking action. Before you settle back into the complacency that lulls you into believing you have forever to do the things you want, use this sharper image of your own limited lifetime to forge ahead with new projects and new directions. *Just make sure you take these new directions after some consideration of your emotional state.*

The best way to find the balance between impulsiveness based on the avoidance of the pain of grieving and the desire to move in new directions is to write down what you want to do but refrain from taking action until *at least six months* have passed after your parent's death. Small indulgences where little is at risk need not wait that long. But big changes, requiring big risks, such as moving to a new residence, leaving a marriage, or changing jobs, should probably wait until a year following your parent's death.

At the one-year anniversary of your parent's death, mark the occasion in some special way. Some religions build into their accepted ritual some form of observance at the one-year mark. Take some time on this day to think about what has happened to you over the last year, as well as how your parent continues to influence your life. Consider how your relationship to your parent has changed since his or her death. And do something that is meaningful to you that will honor your memory of your parent.

It's common that at the one-year point, adult children are feeling re-engaged in their lives and ready to give up their grieving, at least the more obvious signs of it. If you find that you are still unable to move on with your life at this point, consider getting some professional help, as it may indicate that you are experiencing complicated bereavement.

Don't be surprised if you notice that at least once per day *for the rest of your life* you have some sort of thought related to your parent. It may be your parent's voice reminding you of a certain value or way of doing something. Or it may be offering support when you need it through an encouraging word. Allow yourself to take in the words you hear from your parent, as you form a progressively deeper spiritual relationship as the years pass.

CONCLUSION

Throughout this book, I have tried to show how and why the inheritance taboo has needlessly split up families. I have offered concepts and tools to confront the taboo, showing how the bad blood resulting from our inability to face death, dying, and inheritance more directly is something that doesn't have to happen.

For it not to happen, I have suggested that parents must be willing to change their ideas about communicating on the topic. They must be willing to experiment with being more open and direct with their children about their intentions. And they must be willing to accept that dealing with how they want their money and personal possessions distributed after death will be easier and more meaningful for all involved if they begin the process while still alive.

It is time for families to stop thinking that the more secretive they are about inheritance, the less everyone will be hurt. It just isn't true. *It never has been and it never will be.*

Silence and secretiveness have their place in human relationships. But dealing with the money, personal property, and values that one wishes to pass on to one's children is not one of those times where silence and secretiveness works. This has been shown repeatedly over the generations. But because death and dying are so hard to face, we just don't want to learn the lesson and change our behavior. And, of course, it's not made any easier when we are forced to face all the uncomfortable feelings that go with having preferences and making choices.

While I don't expect this book to work miracles in radically changing the nature of how your family relates, I do hope that the ideas and tools presented have at least offered you a map as to another way to deal with this sensitive area of our lives.

Adult children must be willing to go beyond the embarrassment and shame that have been culturally sanctioned in dealing with inheritance. They must be able to face inheritance issues directly, just as they do when they are forced to help their parents with financial and medical concerns. It's time for us to see that the transfer of money and possessions from one generation to the next does not have to be secretive or filled with guilt.

I have emphasized the power of dealing with inheritance issues early and proactively, before a parent is sick and dying. With a clear mind and strong body, we are best able to lovingly talk to our children about our values, make choices regarding medical directives when needed, and discuss how we want our body disposed of and how we want our possessions distributed.

Far from being some kind of morbid exercise, giving away some of our possessions to our children and other family members is one of the most freeing and loving things that we can do in the service of letting go of this world. It's freeing because it begins our process of letting go of our attachment to the material world. In slowly letting go of the material world, we begin to let go of our attachment to our body, individuality, and life itself. Is there anything more powerful than this in preparation for our death?

No matter what religious or spiritual beliefs we may have, we must all let go of everything we have managed to accumulate over a lifetime. Consciously and purposely handing the possessions we are ready to part with to our children is a good start on lessening our attachment to the material world. And the joy that may accompany this giving is an added benefit.

My emphasis has been on helping you see that self-insight is the best tool for confronting the inheritance taboo. The dramas that you enact with parents, siblings, and other family members will *always* be repetitions of the past. No matter how much it may feel like you are dealing directly with your siblings in the here and now around inheritance issues, unencumbered by your past relationship, that will *never* be what is actually occurring. So don't fool yourself about the power of the past, or you will have no idea what hit you. And make no mistake about it, it *will* hit you.

When you begin to tune in to the roles played in families, and how past family dynamics are conditioning your emotions and behavior as you deal with inheritance issues, you are in the position to use this awareness to stop the past from repeating itself and begin new ways of relating.

May you find these new ways, breaking free from the past, so that not only will you negotiate the death of your parents and the inheritance process, but also end up closer to your sibs. And may you shine in the light of the new awakening and possibilities that come when you break through and overcome the inheritance taboo.

REFERENCES

BOOKS

Baines, Barry K. *Ethical Wills: Putting Your Values on Paper* (New York: Perseus, 2002).

Condon, Gerald M., and Jeffrey L. Condon. *Beyond the Grave* (New York: HarperBusiness, 2001).

Hendlin, Steven J. *When Good Enough Is Never Enough: Escaping the Perfection Trap* (New York: Tarcher/Putnam, 1992).

Kennedy, Alexandra. *Losing a Parent: Passage to a New Way of Living* (San Francisco: Harper, 1991).

Pollan, Stephen M., and M. Levine. *Die Broke* (New York: HarperBusiness, 1997).

———. *Second Acts* (New York: HarperCollins, 2003).

ONLINE BABY BOOMER REFERENCE SITES

http://www.bbhq.com/bomrstat.htm

http://www.suddenlysenior.com/seniorfacts.html

ONLINE REFERENCES FOR ESTATE PLANNING

http://www.netplanning.com/consumer/National Network of Estate Planning Attorneys. This is a good online site for answering questions about estate planning, including planning pitfalls, and a thorough question-and-answer section related to various planning situations.

http://www.estateplanninglinks.com. A comprehensive organization of links to various broad aspects of estate planning, all of which lead to numerous other sites on the following topics: understanding estate planning; forms; advanced planning; laws and government; valuation of property, elder law, tax, probate and living trusts; charitable planning; legal resources and others.

http://www.itslegal.com/index.asp. Another legal information site on estate planning issues; wills and trusts; family law, health, and medical issues; consumer law; personal injury and credit and debt:

Nolo.com: http://www.nolo.com/lawcenter/ency/index.cfm/catID/FD 1795A9-8049-422C-9087838F86A2BC2B. Another comprehensive site that answers questions on estate planning, including the law on who has a right to inherit, choosing an executor, choosing a guardian for children, and helping you write your own will.

The Family Fight: Planning to Avoid It by Barry Fish and Les Kotzer (Toronto: Continental Atlantic Publications, 2002) gives weight to the emotional side of inheritance issues, also from two estate attorneys. Their self-published book may be ordered from this site: http://www.familyfight.com.

ONLINE REFERENCES ON GRIEVING

Stages of Grieving from Elisabeth Kübler-Ross: http://www.elisabeth kublerross.com. See also http://www.near-death.com and look under "experts" for Kübler-Ross.

For a critique of Kübler-Ross's stages, see http://www.bereavement.org/e
  kubler-ross.htm.
For a sample of sites that explain healthy grieving and give help, see:
  http://depts.washington.edu/scc/grief.html
  http://www.mtech.edu/counseling/healthygrieving.htm
  http://www.alexandrakennedy.com/

INDEX

ABOUT THE AUTHOR

Don Romero

Steven J. Hendlin, Ph.D., is a licensed clinical psychologist who has been in private practice for twenty-five years. In addition to managing his clinical practice, he writes frequently about investing and the psychology of investing. Besides running his general practice, he works as a sports psychologist with professional and amateur golfers, and as a coach for professional stock traders.